Cooking with Angels

Julie Abbinante
AND M.J. Smith, R.D.

CHRONIMED
PUBLISHING

D1399661

Cooking With Angels ©1995 by Julie Abbinante and M.J. Smith, R.D.

All rights reserved. Except for brief passages for review purposes, no part of this publication may be reproduced, stored in a retrieval system, or transmitted, in any form or by any means, electronic, photocopying, recording, or otherwise, without the prior written permission of Chronimed Publishing.

Library of Congress Cataloging-in-Publication Data

Julie Abbinante and M.J. Smith, R.D.

Cooking With Angels / Julie Abbinante and M.J. Smith, R.D.

p.   cm.

Includes index

ISBN 1-56561-065-2; $12.95

1. Low-fat diet — Recipes
I. Julie Abbinante and M.J. Smith, R.D.
II. Cooking With Angels

Edited by: Jolene Steffer and Jeff Braun
Cover Design: Garborg Design Works
Text Design: Liana Vaiciulis Raudys
Production Artist: Janet Hogge
Art/Production Manager: Claire Lewis
Printed in the United States of America

Published by
Chronimed Publishing
P.O. Box 59032
Minneapolis, MN 55459-9686

10 9 8 7 6 5 4 3 2 1

DEDICATION

This book is dedicated to my own little angel on earth, Danny.

-Julie Abbinante

ACKNOWLEDGMENTS

There were many "angels" serving to get this book to the presses.

I'd like to thank the following people for their help, inspiration, and support: Phyllis Hedges, Celeste Kukla, David Wexler, Jeff Braun, Janet Hogge, Jon Ebersole, and everyone at Chronimed Publishing.

Many thanks to those who provided help in the area of ideas, suggestions, and recipe testing: Barbara Abbinante, Sarah Kipp, Lee Schneider, Brian Hanson, Jennifer Hill, Sandy Hintz, Claire Lewis, and Stephanie Graves.

And then there were others who put their mouths and stomachs on the line to taste-test: the folks at UNCO Data Systems and Chronimed Publishing.

And finally, my unending gratitude to M.J. Smith without whose support, frankness, and assistance this book would not have come true.

To all of you, my heartfelt thanks! This book was blessed to have angels like you!

-Julie Abbinante

NOTICE: CONSULT HEALTH CARE PROFESSIONAL

Readers are advised to seek the guidance of a licensed physician or health care professional before making any changes in a prescribed diet or health care regimen, as each individual case or need may vary. This book is intended for informational purposes only and is not for use as an alternative to appropriate medical care. While every effort has been made to ensure that the information is the most current available, new research findings, being released with increased frequency, may invalidate some data.

Table of Contents

TABLE OF CONTENTS

Cooking With Angels is a collection of heavenly recipes combined with glorious verse. Take this book out on a rainy night or a sunny morning and fill your kitchen with blessed tastes and smells . . . or share the book with someone who needs a visit from an angel.

A "food exchange" value is included for each recipe and is based on the *Exchange List for Meal Planning*, a system developed and published by the American Dietetic Association and the American Diabetes Association.

Angels on High

TIPS FOR HIGH ALTITUDE COOKING

o angel cookbook would be complete without tips for those living especially close to the angels — in higher altitudes.

Many recipes, cooking times, and temperatures need to be changed for altitudes 3,000 feet (914 meters) above sea level or higher. Even if you live 1,000 feet above sea level, it's a good idea to experiment with ingredients and to use the tips below. Then keep records of the changed amounts for future use.

STOVETOP COOKING: Due to the thinner air and lower atmospheric pressure, water, soups, sauces, and other liquids boil at lower temperatures than they would at sea level. So even though your soup is boiling, it will need to boil longer to get hot. However, don't increase the heat; your food might scorch.

FREEZING: When heating or blanching your vegetables before freezing, heat one minute longer than you would at sea level for altitudes of 5,000 feet (1,524 meters) or more.

BREADS: The leavening gases in breads (and cakes) begin to expand more, shortening the time it takes them to rise. The flavor depends in part on the length of the rising time. To maintain that crucial step, and to ensure maximum flavor, just punch the dough down twice before baking. Since flour is drier and able to absorb more liquid in higher climates, your dough needs less flour to achieve proper consistency.

CAKES: Above 3,000 feet, most cakes will fall. To avoid this, decrease the amount of baking powder by 1/8 to 1/4 teaspoon and increase the baking temperature 15 to 25 degrees Fahrenheit (8.3 to 13.9 degrees Celsius). Decreasing the sugar by one to three tablespoons and increasing the liquid by one to four tablespoons also helps.

ANGEL FOOD CAKES: Air is the leavening gas for angel food and sponge cakes. So don't beat too much air into the egg whites — just until they form peaks that fall over. If they become stiff and dry, there's too much air and your cakes may over expand. Also, use less sugar, more flour, and bake at a higher temperature.

COOKIES: Usually, cookies are unaffected by higher altitudes. But you may improve them by slightly increasing baking temperature, decreasing baking powder or soda, increasing liquids and flour, and decreasing the fat and sugar.

MUFFINS, BISCUITS, AND QUICK BREADS: The texture of muffins and biscuits won't change in high altitudes, but they may taste bitter or alkaline. To improve results, slightly reduce the baking soda or powder. When baking quick breads with a cake-like texture, just follow the above recommendations for cakes.

If you'd like to spread your wings further and get more information on high altitude cooking, call or write:

Cooperative Extension Service
Colorado State University
Fort Collins, CO 80523
970-491-7334

Beverages

"Be not forgetful to entertain strangers,
for thereby some have
entertained angels unawares."

-*Hebrews 13:2*

Christmas Eve Eggnog

Use a pretty Christmas punch cup for this elegant beverage.

8 servings—4 ounces each

6 eggs, separated, or 2 c. liquid egg substitute
   plus 6 egg whites
2 Tbsp. sugar
2 c. skim milk
2 tsp. rum flavoring
Garnish: nutmeg

In a large mixing bowl, beat the yolks or egg substitute well, then gradually beat in the sugar. Add the milk slowly, beating constantly. Add the rum flavoring. In a medium mixing bowl, beat egg whites until stiff, then carefully fold into the egg mixture. Fill 8 punch cups, and garnish with nutmeg.

Nutrients per serving:

Calories 89; Fat 4 gm; Cholesterol 161 mg with egg, 2 mg with egg substitute; Sodium 79 mg; Food exchange value: 1/2 skim milk, 1 fat

"Ethereal minstrel! Pilgrim of the sky."

-William Wordsworth

Preacher's Julep

8 servings—8 ounces each

2 c. fresh mint, chopped fine
2 lemons
1 1/2 c. sugar
1 qt. water
1 qt. iced tea

Place chopped mint in a 1-quart pitcher. Peel the lemons, and shred the rind over the mint. In a saucepan, combine the sugar, water, and juice of both lemons. Bring the mixture to a boil, then remove from the heat, and pour over the mint and lemon rind. Allow the mixture to cool to room temperature, then strain off the liquid into a 2 qt. pitcher. Add 1 qt. of your favorite iced tea, and refrigerate until serving time.

Nutrients per serving:
Calories 145; Fat 0; Cholesterol 0; Sodium 8 mg;
Food exchange value: 2 1/2 fruit

"When the Son of Man comes as King
and all the angels with him,
he will sit on his royal throne."

-*Matthew 25:31*

Victorian Iced Tea

8 servings — 8 ounces each

1 c. water
2 Tbsp. sugar
3 whole cloves
2 cinnamon sticks
3 tea bags
2 c. apricot nectar
1/4 c. frozen orange juice concentrate
Garnish: cinnamon sticks or fresh apricot

In a medium saucepan, combine water, sugar, cloves, cinnamon, and tea bags. Simmer for 5 minutes, then remove from heat, and cool at room temperature for 15 minutes. Transfer the tea mixture to a 2-quart pitcher, and add nectar and orange juice concentrate. Stir, then refrigerate.

When ready to serve, pour 4 ounces of the tea mixture over 2 ice cubes in an iced tea glass, and fill with 4 ounces of club soda. Garnish with a fresh apricot wedge or cinnamon stick if desired.

Nutrients per serving:
Calories 62; Fat 0; Cholesterol 0; Sodium 3 mg;
Food exchange value: 1 fruit

"How sweetly did they float
upon the wings
of silence through
the empty-vaulted night. . . ."

—John Milton, Comus

Chamomile Tea

*You'll remember this soothing drink for fallen angel, Peter Rabbit.
Chamomile flowers, which resemble daisies, can usually be found
where dried flowers are sold.*
8 servings — 5 ounces each

1 1/2 qt. boiling water
3 Tbsp. dried chamomile flowers
Honey (optional)

Pour hot water over the flowers in a pretty teapot, and steep for at
least 5 minutes. Strain, and sweeten with honey if desired.

Nutrients per serving:
*Calories 0; Fat 0; Cholesterol 0; Sodium 0;
Food exchange value: Free food*

"Every man contemplates an
angel in his future self."

-Ralph Waldo Emerson

Banana Flight

Are your bananas going brown? Try this angelic remedy.

1 gallon or 16 8-ounce servings

4 bananas, mashed smooth
2 c. orange juice
46-oz. can pineapple juice
2-qt. bottle sugar-free lemon-lime soft drink

Mix bananas, orange juice, and pineapple juice together in a plastic freezer-safe container. Freeze until slushy. Remove from the freezer, and spoon 4 ounces of banana slush into a glass. Top with 4 ounces of soft drink.

Nutrients per serving:
Calories 84; Fat 0; Cholesterol 0; Sodium 21 mg;
Food exchange value: 1 1/2 fruit

"Praise him, all his angels,
all his heavenly armies!"

-Psalms 148:2

Hark the Herald Punch

Serve this punch along with Christmas carols.

1 gallon or 16 8-ounce servings

Juice of 5 large oranges
Juice of 4 large lemons
1 pt. raspberry sherbet
1 pt. pineapple sherbet
2-qt. bottle sugar-free lemon-lime soft drink

Combine juices in a punch bowl. Stir in sherbets. Add soft drink just before serving.

Nutrients per serving:

Calories 93; Fat 1 gm; Cholesterol 3 mg; Sodium 20 mg;
Food exchange value: 1 1/2 fruit

"An angel! Or if not,
an earthly paragon!"

-William Shakespeare, Cymbeline

Bell Ringer Peach Cooler

8 servings—6 ounces each

2 large ripe peaches, with peeling, cut into slices
12 oz. frozen limeade concentrate
2 c. crushed ice
1 Tbsp. rum flavoring

Combine ingredients in a blender. Process until no chunks of peach remain. Serve immediately.

Nutrients per serving:
Calories 86; Fat 0; Cholesterol 0; Sodium 5 mg;
Food exchange value: 1 1/2 fruit

"It is to those who perceive through symbols,
the poets, the artists, and seekers for meaning,
that the angel makes himself known."

-*Theodora Ward*

Perky Angel Punch

8 servings — 5 ounces each

2 c. pineapple juice (may substitute orange juice)
2 c. water
2 c. cranberry juice (may substitute cran-raspberry)
1 Tbsp. whole cloves
4 cinnamon sticks, broken into pieces
1 1/2 tsp. whole allspice
2 Tbsp. brown sugar
1/4 tsp. salt

Combine the first three ingredients in a 12-cup percolator. Place spices, sugar, and salt in the basket. Perk for 10 minutes.

Nutrients per serving:
Calories 85; Fat 0; Cholesterol 0; Sodium 5 mg;
Food exchange value: 1 1/2 fruit

Appetizers

"We trust in plumed procession
For such the angels go—
Rank after Rank, with even feet—
And uniforms of Snow."

-*Emily Dickinson,*
To Fight Aloud, Is Very Brave

Happy Landing Vegetable Dip

12 servings — 1/4 cup each

8 oz. reduced-fat cheddar cheese, shredded
4 oz. fat-free cream cheese, at room temperature
1/4 tsp. dry mustard
1/4 tsp. minced garlic
4 dashes hot sauce
1/2 tsp. Worcestershire sauce
1/2 c. dark beer or nonalcoholic malt beverage
Garnish: sprinkle of paprika

Combine cheeses and seasonings in a food processor. Process 30 seconds to blend. With the processor running on low, add the beer gradually, blending until smooth. Transfer to a serving bowl, and chill at least an hour. Garnish with paprika, and serve with fresh veggie dippers, pretzels, or bread sticks.

Nutrients per serving:

Calories 63; Fat 3 gm; Cholesterol 13 mg; Sodium 149 mg; Food exchange value: 1 lean meat

"O welcome pure-ey'd Faith,
white-handed Hope, Thou hovering angels
girt with golden wings."

-John Milton

Cherub's
Cheese 'n Bean Dip

16 servings — 1/3 cup each

8 oz. nonfat cream cheese, softened
2 16-oz. cans red chili (hot) beans
1/2 c. shredded low-fat cheddar cheese
3 1/2-oz. can diced green chili peppers (chopped)

Spread cream cheese on the bottom of a 9" x 13" pan. Drain the liquid from the beans, and then spread the beans over the cream cheese layer. Sprinkle the cheese over the beans. Scatter the green chilies over the cheese.

Bake in a 350° oven for 15 minutes. Allow to cool slightly (5 to 10 minutes) before serving.

Serve with crackers or low-sodium tortilla chips.

Nutrients per serving:
Calories 90; Fat 2 gm; Cholesterol 8 mg; Sodium: 458 mg;
Food exchange value: 1 bread/starch

> "The delight of the wisdom
> of the angels is to communicate to
> others what they know."
> *-Emanuel Swedenborg*

Saintly Spinach Cheese Squares

24 appetizers—2-inch squares each

Vegetable oil cooking spray
3/4 c. egg substitute
1 c. flour
1 tsp. salt
1 tsp. baking powder
2/3 c. skim milk
3 cloves garlic, crushed
1 c. shredded mozzarella cheese (4 oz.)
10-oz. package frozen chopped spinach,
    thawed and drained

Preheat the oven to 350°. Spray the bottom and sides of a 9" x 13" pan with cooking spray. In a large bowl, combine the egg substitute, flour, salt, baking powder, milk, and garlic. Blend well. Add cheese and spinach. Mix gently, but thoroughly.

Spread the mixture in the pan, and bake for 35 minutes. Cool in the pan for 20 minutes. Cut into squares, and serve.

Nutrients per serving:
Calories 44; Fat 2 gm; Cholesterol 2 mg; Sodium 158 mg;
Food exchange value: 2 vegetable

"Angels and ministers of grace defend us!"
-*William Shakespeare, Hamlet*

Angelic Red Pepper and Zucchini Appetizers

24 appetizers — 2-inch squares each

Vegetable oil cooking spray
2 c. zucchini, thinly sliced with peeling
1 c. diced red bell pepper
1 c. reduced-fat biscuit mix
1/2 c. chopped red onion
1/4 c. grated Parmesan cheese
2 Tbsp. snipped parsley
1/2 tsp. salt
1 tsp. no-salt seasoning
1 tsp. summer savory
1/2 tsp. ground cumin
1 clove garlic, minced
1 c. egg substitute

Preheat oven to 350°. Spray the bottom and sides of a 9" x 13" pan with cooking spray. Combine all ingredients in a large bowl; mix well. Pour the batter into the prepared pan.

Bake for 25 minutes, or until golden brown. Cut into squares.

Nutrients per serving:

Calories 56; Fat 2 gm; Cholesterol 2 mg; Sodium 184 mg;
Food exchange value: 2 vegetable

"Angels can fly because they take
themselves lightly."
–Scottish saying

Radiant Radish Dip

8 servings — 1/4 cup (4 tablespoons) each

1 c. finely chopped radishes
4 oz. nonfat cream cheese
1 clove garlic, minced
1 Tbsp. lemon juice
1 tsp. no-salt seasoning
1/2 tsp. dill weed
2 Tbsp. horseradish sauce
Garnish: parsley sprigs and radishes

Combine all ingredients in a medium bowl; blend well. Turn out into a serving bowl. Chill at least 4 hours before serving.

Garnish with parsley sprigs and radish slices. Serve with water crackers or reduced-sodium biscuits.

Nutrients per serving:

Calories 60; Fat 2 gm; Cholesterol 5 mg; Sodium 201 mg;
Food exchange value: 1 vegetable, 1/2 skim milk

"He had seen angels many times before."

—Mark Helprin,
A Soldier of the Great War

Cucumber Dip
on High

8 servings—2 tablespoons each

8-oz. package nonfat cream cheese, softened
1/2 c. reduced-fat sour cream
1 Tbsp. skim milk
1/4 tsp. reduced-sodium Worcestershire sauce
1/4 tsp. dried dill weed
1 tsp. snipped chives
1/3 c. finely chopped cucumber
Garnish: 1 lemon, quartered

In a medium bowl, combine cream cheese, sour cream, milk,
Worcestershire sauce, dill weed, and chives. Mix until well blended.
Stir in cucumbers. Spoon into a serving dish, and garnish with 4
lemon wedges placed in the center, tips pointing out, sunburst fashion.

Chill several hours or overnight. Serve with assorted chopped fresh
vegetables.

Nutrients per serving:
Calories 18; Fat 0; Cholesterol 0; Sodium 12 mg;
Food exchange value: Free food

"The king said, 'Praise the God
of Shadrach, Meshach, and Abednego!
He sent his angel and rescued these men
who serve and trust him.'"

-Daniel 3:28

Glorious Shrimp Dill Dip

8 servings — 1/4 cup each

1/4 c. 50% reduced-fat sour cream
8-oz. package nonfat cream cheese
1 lemon, halved lengthwise
2 Tbsp. finely chopped onion
1/2 tsp. salt
2 tsp. dried dill weed
1/2 tsp. Tabasco sauce
1 c. finely chopped cooked shrimp

In a medium bowl, blend the sour cream, cream cheese, and juice from half of the lemon until smooth. Add the onion, salt, dill weed, and Tabasco. Mix well. Stir in shrimp. Spoon into a serving bowl, and chill for at least 2 hours to stiffen.

Cut the remaining lemon half in half again, lengthwise. Place the wedges in the middle of the dip to form a *v*, or angel wings. Dust with an additional dash of dill weed, if desired.

Nutrients per serving:

*Calories 36; Fat 1 gm.; Cholesterol 19 mg.; Sodium 239 mg.;
Food exchange value: 1/2 lean meat*

"Outside the open window
The morning air is all awash with angels."
-*Richard Wilbur,*
Love Calls Us to the Things of This World

Heaven-Sent
Herb Cheese Dip

6 servings — 1/4 cup each

8 oz. nonfat cream cheese
1/2 c. nonfat mayonnaise
1/2 c. grated onion
1/2 tsp. garlic powder
1 tsp. dry mustard
1 tsp. celery seed
1/8 tsp. cayenne pepper
1/2 tsp. white wine Worcestershire sauce

Combine all ingredients in a medium mixing bowl. Blend thoroughly. Refrigerate for at least an hour before serving.

Serve with raw vegetables such as carrots, celery, cauliflower, and snow peas.

Nutrients per serving:
Calories 43; Fat 0; Cholesterol 2 mg; Sodium 374 mg;
Food exchange value: 1/2 skim milk

Sweet Chariot Curried Turkey Bites

Approximately 60 servings — 1 piece each

4 medium turkey breast tenderloins (3 lb.)
1 c. nonfat sour cream
2 Tbsp. lemon juice
2 tsp. curry powder
2 tsp. salt
1/4 tsp. black pepper
2 tsp. reduced-sodium soy sauce
2 cloves garlic, minced

Vegetable oil cooking spray
2 Tbsp. caraway seeds (optional)

Sauce:
1/4 c. dry mustard
2 Tbsp. sugar
1/4 c. cider vinegar
1/2 c. nonfat sour cream
1/8 tsp. salt
1 Tbsp. flour

Day One:

Lay the turkey breasts on a flat surface or cutting board. Using the flat side of a meat mallet, pound the turkey breasts until they're about 1/2-inch thick. Cut away the white gristle down the middle of each breast, leaving each breast in two pieces. Cut each breast portion into 1-inch triangles, approximately 30 pieces per breast.

In a large bowl, combine the sour cream, lemon juice, curry powder, salt, pepper, soy sauce, and garlic. Mix well. Add the turkey breast triangles to the cream mixture. Cover and refrigerate overnight.

Day Two:

Preheat the oven to 350°. Spray two 15" x 10" jelly roll pans with cooking spray. Place 30 pieces of turkey in each pan. Sprinkle evenly with caraway seeds (if desired). Bake for 25 to 30 minutes, until turkey begins to brown slightly and curry mixture is just dry.

While the turkey is baking, combine the sauce ingredients. Spoon into a serving bowl, and refrigerate. When the turkey is done, spoon turkey pieces onto a platter, and serve warm with mustard sauce.

Nutrients per serving:
Calories 39; Fat <1 g; Cholesterol 14 mg; Sodium 119 mg;
Food exchange value: 1/2 lean meat

"Maybe other angels have dropped into
other Elm Street backyards? . . . Folks keep
so much of the best stuff quiet, don't they."
-*Allan Gurganus,*
It Had Wings

Paradise Parmesan Biscuit Wings

60 servings — 1 wing each

Vegetable oil cooking spray
3 cans refrigerator buttermilk biscuits
   (30 biscuits)
1/3 c. canola oil
2 tsp. garlic powder
1 Tbsp. oregano
1/4 c. Parmesan cheese

Preheat oven to 425°. Spray a cookie sheet with cooking spray. Cut each biscuit in half. Stretch each half lengthwise, then twist and cross ends over so they stick out like wings. Place on the cookie sheet. Bake for 4 minutes.

Combine the remaining ingredients. As soon as "wings" come out of the oven, place them in the cheese and oil mixture. Toss to coat well. Return wings to the cookie sheet, and bake for an additional 4 to 5 minutes, or until golden brown. Serve warm or cooled.

Nutrients per serving:
Calories 31; Fat 1 gm; Cholesterol 0; Sodium 91 mg;
Food exchange value: 1/2 bread/starch

"Like living flame their faces
seemed to glow.
Their wings were gold.
And all their bodies shone more
dazzling white than any earthly show."

-*Dante Alighieri,*
The Paradiso

Pearly Gates
Onion Cheese Puffs

Approximately 50 servings—1 puff each

2 jars Holland-style white onions
2 1/2 c. shredded reduced-fat cheddar cheese
   (10 oz.)
1/2 c. + 2 Tbsp. nonfat sour cream
2 Tbsp. margarine, softened
2 c. flour
3/4 tsp. salt
1 1/2 tsp. paprika

Preheat oven to 400°. Drain onions thoroughly in a colander. Lightly pat with a paper towel. Blend the cheese with the sour cream and margarine. Stir in the flour, salt, and paprika. Mix well. Flatten 2 teaspoons of dough in your hand, and wrap the dough around an onion, covering the onion completely. Repeat until all the onions are wrapped. Place on an ungreased baking sheet. Bake for 10 to 15 minutes. Serve warm or cooled.

Tip: This recipe can be prepared early in the day and refrigerated. Add 2 to 3 minutes to baking time.

Nutrients per serving:
Calories 45; Fat 1 gm; Cholesterol 4 mg; Sodium 145 mg;
Food exchange value: 1/2 bread/starch

Breakfasts & Breads

"The guardian angels of life sometimes fly so
high as to be beyond our sight,
but they are always looking down upon us."

-Jean Paul Richter

Morning Glory Muffins
24 servings — 1 muffin each

2 c. flour
1 c. cornmeal
5 tsp. baking powder
1 tsp. salt
2/3 c. sugar
1/2 c. vegetable oil
2 eggs or 1/2 c. liquid egg substitute
1/2 c. orange juice concentrate
1 c. skim milk
7-oz. can crushed pineapple, drained well
1/2 c. grated carrots

Preheat oven to 425°. In a mixing bowl, combine the first four ingredients, and mix well. In another mixing bowl, beat the sugar, oil, eggs, orange juice concentrate, and skim milk until smooth. Make a well in the dry ingredients, and pour in the egg and oil mixture. Stir just until moist. Gently fold in the drained pineapple and grated carrots.

Line muffin tins with liners, and divide muffin batter among 24 cups. Bake for 20 to 25 minutes.

Nutrients per serving:

Calories 143; Fat 5 gm; Cholesterol 18 mg with egg, 0 with egg substitute; Sodium 177 mg; Food exchange value: 1 bread/starch, 1 fruit

"How many angels are there?
One—who transforms our life—is plenty."

-Traditional saying

Eternal Pancakes

6 batches of pancakes — 10 4-inch cakes per batch

7 c. flour
2 c. nonfat dry milk powder
1 Tbsp. salt
1/2 c. baking powder
1/2 c. sugar

Combine ingredients in a plastic container and mix well. Cover until ready to use.

To prepare pancake batter, combine 1 1/2 cups of mix with 1 egg, 1 cup of water or fruit juice, and 1 tablespoon of vegetable oil in a mixing bowl. Stir until smooth, then cook in a nonstick skillet coated with cooking spray.

Nutrients per serving:
Calories 94; Fat 2 gm; Cholesterol 22 mg; Sodium 271 mg;
Food exchange value: 1 bread/starch

Easter Egg Nest

1 large ring—cut into 12 pieces

6 raw eggs, in the shell
Food coloring
1/8 c. sugar
12-oz. pkg. Pillsbury® hot roll mix
Grated peel of 1 lemon
1 egg or 1/4 c. liquid egg substitute
Water
Vegetable oil cooking spray
1/4 c. chopped dried fruit
2/3 c. powdered sugar
1-2 Tbsp. lemon juice

Wash the 6 raw eggs. Tint the shells with food coloring, and set aside. In a small mixing bowl, combine sugar, hot roll mix, and grated lemon rind. Stir well. Add 1 egg and water according to package directions. Stir dough, and form into a smooth ball. Cover and let rise in a warm place for 10 minutes.

Spray a nonstick baking sheet with cooking spray. Divide dough in half. Form each half into a 24-inch rope, then braid the ropes together in the shape of a nest. Plant the colored uncooked eggs in the middle of the nest. Carefully place the chopped dried fruit on the dough. Cover, and let rise 30 minutes.

Bake in a preheated 350° oven for 20 to 25 minutes. When bread is cooled, transfer nest and eggs to a serving platter. Mix powdered sugar together with lemon juice in a small bowl, and drizzle over the braid.

Nutrient analysis for nest only:

Calories 129.; Fat 2 gm.; Cholesterol 18 mg with egg, 0 with egg substitute.;
Sodium 148 mg.; Food exchange value: 1 1/2 bread/starch

"Don't you know that I could call on my
Father for help, and at once he would send me
more than twelve armies of angels?"

- Antoine De Saint-Exupery

"I want to be an angel
And with the angels stand,
A crown upon my forehead,
A harp within my hand."
-*Urania Bailey,*
I Want to Be an Angel

Popover Paradise

6 large popovers — 1 popover each

Vegetable oil cooking spray
1 c. skim milk
1 Tbsp. melted margarine
2 eggs or 1/2 c. liquid egg substitute
1 c. flour
1 Tbsp. sugar
1/2 tsp. salt

Preheat oven to 450°. Spray 6 muffin cups with cooking spray, and place in the oven to warm. Combine all ingredients in a medium mixing bowl. Beat with an egg beater just until smooth. Pour batter into hot muffin cups, filling just half full.

Bake for 20 minutes, then reduce heat to 350° and bake for 20 minutes longer. Remove from pan, and serve immediately.

Nutrients per serving:

Calories 141; Fat 4 gm; Cholesterol 72 mg with egg, 1 mg with egg substitute; Sodium 246 mg; Food exchange value: 1 1/2 bread/starch, 1/2 fat

"No one knows, however, when that day and hour will come — neither the angels in heaven nor the son; the Father alone knows."

-Matthew 24:36

Wee Angel Orange Rolls

Thank you, Helen Meder

10 servings — 1 roll each

1 lb. loaf frozen sweet-roll dough
2 Tbsp. melted margarine
1/4 c. sugar
1 tsp. cinnamon

Frosting:
1 c. powdered sugar
Zest of 1 orange (tiny narrow strips of the colored
   part of the orange rind)
1 Tbsp. melted margarine
Juice from 1 orange to thin frosting

Thaw bread dough according to package directions. Roll out on a floured surface to a 14" x 8" rectangle. Spread dough with melted margarine, then sprinkle with sugar and cinnamon. Roll up dough, and pinch shut. Cut rolls into 1 1/2-inch pieces, and arrange in a 9-inch round baking pan coated with cooking spray. Cover rolls, and allow to rise about 2 1/2 inches high.

Bake in a preheated 350° oven for 20 to 25 minutes. Combine frosting ingredients in a small mixing bowl. Spread frosting over the rolls while they are still warm.

Nutrients per serving:
Calories 212; Fat 4 gm; Cholesterol 0; Sodium 253 mg;
Food exchange value: 2 bread/starch, 1/2 fruit, 1/2 fat

Hawaiian Angel Bread

20 servings—1 slice each

Vegetable oil cooking spray
1/4 c. dried coconut
3 c. flour
1/2 c. sugar
2/3 c. brown sugar
1 tsp. salt
1 tsp. soda
1 tsp. cinnamon
1/4 c. chopped macadamia nuts (may substitute
    walnuts)
2 tsp. vanilla
3 eggs or 3/4 c. liquid egg substitute
1/3 c. vegetable oil
1 c. nonfat sour cream
2 c. mashed ripe bananas

Preheat oven to 350°. Spray a Bundt cake pan with cooking spray.
(If you don't have a Bundt pan, substitute 2 loaf pans.) Dust with
flour, and sprinkle the bottom of the pan with dried coconut.
Combine all remaining ingredients in a large mixing bowl, and beat
until smooth. Pour batter into the prepared pan, and bake for 50 to
60 minutes, or until the cake tests done. Cool for 15 minutes, then
remove to a rack to cool completely.

Nutrients per serving:

Calories 202; Fat 6 gm; Cholesterol 32 mg; Sodium 200 mg;
Food exchange value: 2 bread/starch, 1 fat

"How like an angel came I down!
How bright are all things here!
When first among his works I did appear,
Oh, how their glory did me crown!"

-Thomas Traherne,
Wonder

Eternal Bran Muffins

60 servings — 1 muffin each

2 c. apple juice, boiling
2 c. All Bran cereal
1 c. margarine
2 1/2 c. sugar
4 eggs or 1 c. liquid egg substitute
4 c. buttermilk
4 c. Bran Buds cereal
6 c. flour
5 tsp. soda

Preheat oven to 400°. Pour boiling apple juice over All Bran in a medium bowl. Let stand for several minutes. Select a large plastic bowl with a tight fitting lid for refrigerator storage to complete the recipe. Cream margarine and sugar in the large plastic bowl. Add eggs, one at a time. Add buttermilk, All Bran mixture, and Bran Buds. Mix well. Beat in flour and soda. Spoon into lined muffin cups, and bake for 18 minutes.

This batter lasts for 1 month in the refrigerator. Add raisins or chopped mixed dried fruit to these muffins for variety.

Nutrients per serving:

Calories 147; Fat 4 gm; Cholesterol 14 mg with egg, 0 with egg substitute; Sodium 179 mg; Food exchange value: 1 bread/starch, 1 fruit

"How did he get thar? Angels."

-John Hay, Little Breeches

Tired Angel French Toast

8 servings — 1 slice each

1 Tbsp. margarine
1/4 c. brown sugar
1/2 tsp. cinnamon
1 tsp. grated orange rind
2/3 c. orange juice
4 eggs, slightly beaten, or 1 c. liquid egg substitute
8 slices dried out bread

Preheat oven to 350°. Place a 9" x 13" aluminum cake pan in the oven to warm, about 5 minutes. Remove the cake pan from the oven, and place margarine in the pan. Tilt the pan to melt the margarine over the bottom. Sprinkle sugar and cinnamon evenly over the margarine coating. In a shallow mixing bowl, mix orange rind, orange juice, and eggs. Dip bread into the egg mixture, and arrange in a single layer in the cake pan. Pour remaining egg mixture over the bread.

Bake for 25 to 30 minutes, or until the top is golden brown. Serve with fresh fruit topping and a splash of your favorite syrup.

Nutrients per serving:

Calories 154; Fat 5 gm; Cholesterol 106 mg with egg, 0 with egg substitute; Sodium 169 mg; Food exchange value: 1/2 fruit, 1 bread/starch, 1 fat

Heavenly
Hot Cross Buns

Celebrate Easter with these traditional favorites.

18 servings—1 bun each

1 c. skim milk, scalded
2 Tbsp. margarine
1/4 c. sugar
1 tsp. salt
1 pkg. dry yeast
1 egg, beaten, or 1/4 c. liquid egg substitute
1 tsp. cinnamon
4 1/2 c. flour
3/4 c. raisins
Vegetable oil cooking spray
1 egg, beaten

Powdered sugar frosting:
1 c. powdered sugar
1/2 tsp. vanilla
1 dash salt
2-3 Tbsp. skim milk

Combine 1 cup milk, margarine, sugar, and salt in a large bowl. Cool to lukewarm. Add yeast, and let stand for 3 minutes. Add 1 egg, cinnamon, and flour. Mix in raisins. Let dough rise until doubled in bulk.

Shape into large round biscuits. Place 1 inch apart on a baking pan sprayed with cooking spray. Cover and let rise until double in bulk.

Preheat oven to 400°. Brush dough with egg, and bake for 20 minutes. Cool, then remove buns to a wire rack. Prepare frosting in a small bowl, and drizzle over each bun in a cross pattern.

Nutrients per serving:

Calories 193; Fat 2 gm; Cholesterol 12 mg with egg, 0 with egg substitute; Sodium 130 mg; Food exchange value: 2 1/2 bread/starch

Angel Filled Pumpkin Bread

32 servings — 1 slice each

Vegetable oil cooking spray
1 c. brown sugar
1 c. white sugar
2/3 c. vegetable oil
1/2 c. orange juice
16-oz. can pumpkin
3 eggs or 3/4 c. liquid egg substitute
3 c. flour
2 tsp. baking soda
1 1/2 tsp. cinnamon
1/2 tsp. salt
1/2 tsp. ginger
1/2 tsp. nutmeg

Filling:

1/3 c. brown sugar
1 c. nonfat sour cream
4 oz. fat-free cream cheese, softened to room
　　temperature
1 egg or 1/4 c. liquid egg substitute

Preheat oven to 350°. Spray 2 loaf pans with cooking spray. Combine sugars, oil, orange juice, pumpkin, and eggs in a large mixing bowl, and beat well. Add remaining ingredients, and beat well. In a small mixing bowl, combine ingredients for the filling. Divide half of the pumpkin batter between the 2 prepared loaf pans. Spread the filling over the batter, then top with the remaining batter. Bake for 1 hour or until bread tests done.

Nutrients per serving:

Calories 165; Fat 5 gm; Cholesterol 27 mg; Sodium 134 mg;
Food exchange value: 1 bread/starch, 1 fat, 1/2 fruit

Heavenly Nut Bread
18 servings — 1 slice each

Vegetable oil cooking spray
3 c. all-purpose flour
1/2 c. sugar
1 Tbsp. baking powder
1/2 tsp. salt
1 Tbsp. dried basil
1/4 tsp. baking soda
1 egg, beaten
12-oz. can evaporated skim milk
1/4 c. canola oil
1 c. (4 oz.) shredded reduced-fat mozzarella cheese
1/2 c. pine nuts (pignoli), optional

Preheat oven to 350°. Spray the bottom and sides of a loaf pan with cooking spray. Stir together dry ingredients in a medium mixing bowl. In a separate bowl, combine egg, milk, oil, and cheese. Add the egg mixture to the dry ingredients, and blend well. Stir in nuts, if desired. Pour batter into the loaf pan. Bake for 50 to 60 minutes, or until a toothpick inserted near the center comes out clean.

Cool in the pan for 10 minutes. Turn out onto a wire rack and cool thoroughly. For the best flavor, wrap and store overnight before slicing.

Nutrients per serving (without nuts):

*Calories 180; Fat 9 gm; Cholesterol 16 mg; Sodium 214 mg;
Food exchange value: 1 1/2 bread/starch, 1 fat*

"How many angels can dance
on the point of a very fine needle
without jostling each other?"

Isaac D'Israeli, Curiosities of Literature

Berry Divine Muffins
12 servings — 1 muffin each

1 1/2 c. all-purpose flour
2/3 c. sugar
2 tsp. baking powder
2 tsp. vanilla extract
1 egg
1/4 c. + 2 Tbsp. skim milk
1/2 c. nonfat sour cream
1/4 c. canola oil
3/4 c. fresh or frozen (thawed) berries (blueberries,
    raspberries, or blackberries)

Preheat the oven to 400°. Combine the flour, sugar, and baking powder in a large mixing bowl. In a separate bowl, combine the vanilla, egg, milk, sour cream, and oil. Add the egg mixture to the dry ingredients. Blend just until moistened. (Batter will be slightly lumpy.) Gently fold in berries.

Fill paper-lined muffin cups 2/3 full. Bake for 20 to 25 minutes, or until tops are golden brown. Remove from pan, cool, and serve.

Nutrients per serving:
Calories 162; Fat 5 gm; Cholesterol 18 mg; Sodium 105 mg;
Food exchange value: 1 bread/starch, 1/2 fruit, 1 fat

Caraway Up to Heaven Bread

6 servings — 1 wedge each

Vegetable oil cooking spray
1 pkg. quick-rise yeast
1/4 c. warm water
1 c. nonfat cottage cheese
1/4 c. sugar
1 Tbsp. onion powder
1 Tbsp. margarine, melted
1 Tbsp. caraway seed
1 tsp. salt
1/4 tsp. baking soda
1 egg
1 c. all-purpose flour

Spray an 8" round casserole with cooking spray. Soften the yeast in the warm water. In a large mixing bowl, combine cottage cheese, sugar, onion powder, margarine, caraway seed, salt, baking soda, egg, and softened yeast. Add flour to form a stiff dough. Cover the bowl and let dough rise in a warm place until it expands half again in size (about 30 minutes).

Stir down the dough, and turn out into the prepared casserole. Cover and let dough rise an additional 20 minutes.

Bake, uncovered, at 350° for 30 to 40 minutes. Cut into 6 wedges. Serve warm or cooled.

Nutrients per serving:

Calories 171; Fat 3 gm; Cholesterol 39 mg; Sodium 578 mg; Food exchange value: 2 bread/starch

Adam's Apple Muffin Cake

12 servings — 1 muffin each

2 1/2 c. flour
1 Tbsp. baking powder
1/2 tsp. baking soda
2 Tbsp. cinnamon
1/2 tsp. allspice
1/4 tsp. mace
3/4 c. sugar
2 Tbsp. margarine
1 c. plain nonfat yogurt
1 Tbsp. vanilla extract
2/3 c. applesauce
1/2 c. egg substitute
1 c. finely chopped, peeled apple
Vegetable oil cooking spray

Preheat oven to 350°. In a large bowl, combine the flour, baking powder, baking soda, spices, and sugar.

Melt the margarine in a medium saucepan. Remove from heat. Stir in the yogurt, vanilla, applesauce, and egg substitute. Blend well. Beat the margarine mixture into the dry ingredients, and blend until the batter is smooth. Stir in apple.

Spray the bottom, tube, and sides of an angel food cake pan with cooking spray. Pour batter into the pan. Bake for 50 to 60 minutes, until a toothpick inserted near the center comes out clean.

Cool in the pan for 10 minutes before turning out onto a serving plate. Serve warm or cool.

Nutrients per serving:

*Calories 218; Fat 3 gm; Cholesterol 1 mg; Sodium 286 mg;
Food exchange value: 2 bread/starch, 1/2 fruit, 1/2 fat*

"Instead, you have come to Mount Zion
and to the city of the living God, the heavenly
Jerusalem, with its thousands of angels."

-Hebrews 12:22

Glowing Orange Casserole Bread

12 servings—1 slice each

Vegetable oil cooking spray
1 1/2 c. whole wheat flour
1 c. all-purpose flour
1/2 c. quick-cooking rolled oats
1/3 c. packed brown sugar
2 tsp. baking powder
1/2 tsp. baking soda
1 1/2 c. sour skim milk*
1 egg
1/4 c. orange juice concentrate
1 tsp. orange flavoring
2 Tbsp. sunflower nuts
Honey

*To make sour milk, place 2 tablespoons of lemon juice in a 2-cup measure. Add skim milk to measure 1 1/2 cups.

Preheat oven to 350°. Spray the sides and bottom of a 1 1/2-quart casserole with cooking spray. In a large bowl, combine flours, oats, sugar, baking powder, and baking soda. Add milk, egg, orange juice concentrate, and orange flavoring; stir until ingredients are just moistened. Stir in sunflower nuts.

Pour batter into the prepared casserole. Bake for 40 to 45 minutes, until lightly browned. Cover casserole with foil, and continue baking an additional 10 minutes.

Cool bread in casserole for 15 minutes, then turn out on wire rack. Brush the top of the bread with honey. Serve warm or cooled.

Nutrients per serving:
Calories 133; Fat 2 gm; Cholesterol 18 mg; Sodium 158 mg;
Food exchange value: 1 1/2 bread/starch

"Ye watchers and ye holy ones,
Bright seraphs, cherubim and thrones,
Raise the glad strain: Alleluia!
Cry out, dominions, princedoms, powers,
virtues, archangels, angel choirs: Alleluia!"

–John Athelstan Riley,
Ye Watchers and Ye Holy Ones

Angel's Yogurt Coffee Cake

16 servings — 1 slice each

Vegetable oil cooking spray
3 Tbsp. canola oil
1/2 c. applesauce
1 Tbsp. almond flavoring
1/2 c. granulated sugar
1/2 c. egg substitute
1 c. plain nonfat yogurt
2 c. flour
1 tsp. baking soda
1 tsp. baking powder

Filling:
2 Tbsp. sugar
1 Tbsp. cinnamon

Preheat the oven to 350°. Spray the bottom, tube, and sides of an angel food cake pan with cooking spray. Combine the filling ingredients in a small bowl, and set aside.

In a large bowl, blend together oil, applesauce, almond flavoring, and sugar; beat well. Blend in egg substitute and yogurt. In a medium bowl, sift together flour, baking soda, and baking powder. Add to the egg mixture; beat well.

Pour half of the batter into the prepared pan. Sprinkle the filling evenly over the batter. Pour the remaining batter over the filling.

Bake for 40 to 45 minutes, until a toothpick inserted near the center comes out clean. Cool in the pan for 10 minutes. Turn out on a wire rack or serving plate.

Nutrients per serving:

Calories 154; Fat 5 gm; Cholesterol 0; Sodium 135 mg;
Food exchange value: 1 1/2 bread/starch, 1 1/2 fat

"It will be like this at the end of the age:
the angels will go out and gather up the
evil people from among the good."

-Matthew 13:49

Festive Cranberry-Lemon Bread

18 servings — 1 slice each

Vegetable oil cooking spray
2 c. all-purpose flour
3/4 c. sugar
1 1/2 tsp. baking powder
1/2 tsp. salt
1/2 tsp. baking soda
1/4 c. margarine, softened
1 Tbsp. grated lemon peel
3/4 c. lemonade concentrate
1 egg
1 c. fresh or frozen cranberries
   (thawed and drained), chopped
1/2 c. chopped walnuts

Preheat oven to 350°. Lightly spray the bottom only of a 9" x 5" loaf pan. In a large bowl, mix together flour, sugar, baking powder, salt, and baking soda. Using a fork, cut the margarine into the dry ingredients until mixture is crumbly. Add lemon peel, lemonade concentrate, and egg. Stir until moistened. Fold in cranberries and nuts. Spread into the prepared loaf pan.

Bake 55 to 60 minutes, or until a toothpick inserted near the center comes out clean. Cool in the pan 10 minutes. Remove to a wire rack, and allow to cool completely before slicing.

Note: This bread is best when left covered overnight, before serving, to allow flavors to blend.

Nutrients per serving:

Calories 151; Fat 5 gm; Cholesterol 10 mg; Sodium 149 mg; Food exchange value: 1 bread/starch, 1 fat, 1/2 fruit

"A guardian angel o'er his life presiding,
Doubling his pleasures, and
his cares dividing."

—Samuel Rogers, Human Life

Manna From Heaven
Lemon Bread

18 servings — 1 slice each

Vegetable oil cooking spray
1 c. whole wheat flour
1/3 c. all-purpose flour
2 tsp. baking powder
2 Tbsp. margarine
1/2 c. sugar
3 Tbsp. honey
1 egg
1 egg white
1/2 c. skim milk
Grated rind of one lemon

Glaze:
Juice from one medium lemon
1-2 Tbsp. powdered sugar

Spray a 9" x 5" loaf pan with cooking spray. Preheat oven to 350°. In a medium bowl, sift together flours and baking powder. In a separate bowl, cream together margarine, sugar, and honey. Stir in egg, egg white, milk, and lemon rind. Mix thoroughly with dry ingredients, adding flour mixture 1/2 cup at a time. Pour into the prepared loaf pan, and let stand 20 minutes.

Bake for 40 to 45 minutes. Let stand in the pan on a wire rack for 10 minutes; turn out onto a serving plate.

Mix together lemon juice and powdered sugar. Brush over the top of the warm loaf, and serve.

Nutrients per serving:
*Calories 88; Fat 2 gm; Cholesterol 10 mg; Sodium 126 mg;
Food exchange value: 1 bread/starch*

The Hebrew word for angel is
mal'akh, meaning messenger.

Blissful Banana Bread

18 servings — 1 slice each

8 oz. carton reduced-fat (not nonfat) sour cream
1 c. sugar
1/4 c. margarine, softened but not melted
1 1/4 c. mashed overripe banana (about 3 medium)
2 eggs
2 Tbsp. banana flavoring
2 1/2 c. all-purpose flour
1 1/2 tsp. baking powder
1/2 tsp. baking soda
1/2 c. chopped walnuts (optional)
Vegetable oil cooking spray

Preheat the oven to 350°. In a medium bowl, combine sour cream, sugar, and margarine until well blended. Stir in banana, eggs, and flavoring; mix well. In a large bowl, sift together flour, baking powder, and baking soda. Add banana mixture, and stir together until moistened. Fold in chopped walnuts, if desired.

Spray the bottom and 3/4 up the sides of a 9" x 5" loaf pan with cooking spray. Pour batter into the pan. Bake for 1 hour, or until a toothpick inserted near the center comes out clean.

Cool for 5 minutes, then remove from pan.

Nutrients per serving (without walnuts):
*Calories 153; Fat 3 gm; Cholesterol 0; Sodium 130 mg;
Food exchange value: 2 bread/starch*

Nutrients per serving (with walnuts):
*Calories 173; Fat 5 gm; Cholesterol 0; Sodium 130 mg;
Food exchange value: 2 bread/starch, 1/2 fat*

"Hark! The glad celestial hymn
Angel choirs above are raising;
Cherubim and seraphim,
In unceasing chorus praising,
Fill the heavens with sweet accord:
Holy, holy, holy Lord!"

*Ignaz Franz (translated by Clarence Walworth),
Holy God, We Praise Thy Name*

Golden Raisin/Cardamom Bread

18 servings — 1 slice each

Vegetable oil cooking spray
2 c. water
1 c. golden raisins
2 1/2 c. all-purpose flour
1/2 c. sugar
1 1/4 c. buttermilk
1/3 c. applesauce
1 tsp. baking powder
1/2 tsp. baking soda
1/2 tsp. ground cardamom
1/2 tsp. salt
1/2 c. egg substitute

Preheat the oven to 350°. Spray the bottom only of a 9" x 5" loaf pan with cooking spray. Bring water to boil in a large saucepan. Add raisins, and continue boiling for 1 full minute. Remove from heat, and let stand 10 minutes.

Combine remaining ingredients in a large bowl. Mix well. Drain water from raisins, and fold raisins gently into batter. Pour batter into the prepared loaf pan.

Bake 55 to 60 minutes or until a toothpick inserted near the center comes out clean. Cool for 10 minutes. Remove from pan, and complete cooling on a wire rack before slicing.

Note: This bread is best when left standing overnight to allow flavors to blend.

Nutrients per serving:

Calories 134; Fat 1 gm; Cholesterol 1 mg; Sodium 138 mg;
Food exchange value: 1 1/2 bread/starch

Jacob's Batter
Cheese Bread

10 servings — 1 slice each

Vegetable oil cooking spray
2 c. unbleached flour
1 c. shredded reduced-fat mozzarella cheese
1 Tbsp. no-salt seasoning
1 package quick-rise active dry yeast
3/4 c. skim milk
2 Tbsp. margarine
3/4 c. egg substitute

Preheat oven to 350°. Spray a 1 1/2 to 2-quart casserole with cooking spray. In a large bowl, combine 1 cup of the flour, cheese, seasoning, and yeast; blend well.

In a small saucepan, heat the milk and margarine until very warm, but not scorched. (Margarine does not need to melt completely.) Add the warm liquid and egg substitute to the flour mixture. Mix with a fork until well blended. Stir in the remaining flour to form a stiff dough. Cover the bowl loosely, and let rise in warm place until light and doubled in size (approximately 30 minutes).

Punch down dough to remove air bubbles. Turn into the prepared casserole. Cover and let rise in warm place an additional 35 minutes, or until doubled again in size.

Bake in the casserole for 40 to 45 minutes until bread is a deep golden brown and a toothpick inserted near the center comes out clean.

Remove from casserole immediately. Cool on a wire rack for 15 minutes before slicing.

Nutrients per serving:

Calories 190; Fat 6 gm.; Cholesterol 13 mg.; Sodium 169 mg.;
Food exchange value: 1 1/2 bread/starch, 1/2 skim milk

"God will put his angels in charge of you
to protect you wherever you go."

- Psalms 91:11

Risin' Raisin Almond Loaf

18 servings — 1 slice each

Vegetable oil cooking spray
1 1/2 c. water
1 c. raisins
1/4 c. canola oil
2/3 c. applesauce
1 Tbsp. almond extract
3/4 c. egg substitute
2 1/2 c. all-purpose flour
1 c. sugar
2 tsp. baking powder
1/2 tsp. baking soda
2 tsp. allspice
1/2 tsp. salt
1 c. sliced almonds (optional)
1 Tbsp. powdered sugar (optional)

Preheat the oven to 350°. Spray the bottom and sides of a 9" x 5" loaf pan with cooking spray. Bring water to boiling in a medium saucepan. Remove from heat; stir in raisins. Let stand 15 minutes. Drain, reserving 1/2 cup of water.

In a large bowl, stir together canola oil, applesauce, almond extract, and cooking water reserved from raisins. Add egg substitute, and beat until well blended. Stir in 1 cup of the flour, sugar, baking powder, baking soda, allspice, and salt. Add remaining flour, and stir vigorously to blend well. Fold in raisins. Stir in nuts (if desired).

Pour batter into pan. Bake for 50 to 60 minutes or until a toothpick inserted near the center comes out clean.

Cool in the pan for 15 minutes. Turn loaf out onto a serving plate. Allow loaf to cool, then sprinkle powdered sugar over top, if desired.

Nutrients per serving (without nuts):

Calories 188; Fat 3 gm; Cholesterol 0; Sodium 179 mg;
Food exchange value: 1 1/2 bread/starch, 1 fruit

Nutrients per serving (with nuts):

Calories 262; Fat 10 gm; Cholesterol 0; Sodium 179 mg;
Food exchange value: 1 bread/starch, 1 1/2 fruit, 2 fat

Fly Away Quiche Cups

5 servings—2 quiche cups each

2 slices turkey bacon
8-oz. package nonfat cream cheese
2 Tbsp. skim milk
1/2 c. egg substitute
1/2 c. shredded reduced-fat Swiss cheese
2 Tbsp. chopped green onions
2 tsp. dill weed
Vegetable oil cooking spray
1 can buttermilk refrigerator biscuits (10 biscuits)

Preheat the oven to 375°. Cook turkey bacon in a small skillet until crisp. Remove from skillet to a paper towel, and press dry. Crumble bacon, and set aside. In a small bowl, beat together cream cheese, milk, and egg substitute until smooth. Stir in Swiss cheese, green onions, and dill weed.

Spray 10 cups of a muffin tin with cooking spray. Separate dough into 10 biscuits. Place biscuits in muffin tins. Firmly press each biscuit into the bottom and up the sides of the muffin cup, forming a 1/4-inch rim.

Divide bacon crumbs in half. Sprinkle half evenly among the 10 biscuit cups. Spoon approximately 2 tablespoons of egg mixture into each biscuit-lined cup.

Bake for 20 to 25 minutes, until filling is set. Remove quiche cups from muffin tin, and sprinkle evenly with remaining bacon crumbs.

Nutrients per serving:

Calories 213; Fat 6 gm; Cholesterol 9 mg; Sodium 463 mg;
Food exchange value: 1 1/2 bread/starch, 1 1/2 lean meat

St. Michael is the first angel
to whom the Catholic church granted
a special liturgical observance.

Soups & *Salads*

"Heaven is not reached at a single bound,
but we build the ladder by which we rise."

-Josiah Holland, Gradatim

Choir's Favorite Chicken Salad

8 servings — 1 cup each

1 small pkg. Uncle Ben's rice mix
2 2.5-oz. cans white meat chicken, drained
4 ribs celery, diced
4 green onions, chopped
13-oz. can pineapple tidbits, drained
1/4 c. coconut flakes

Dressing:
1/2 c. reduced-fat mayonnaise
1 Tbsp. lemon juice
1 tsp. curry powder
1/2 tsp. salt
1/2 tsp. pepper

Prepare rice mix according to package directions, and cool.
Meanwhile, in a large salad bowl, combine other ingredients for
salad. In a small mixing bowl, blend ingredients for dressing. Fold
cooled rice and dressing into the chicken and vegetable mixture, and
chill until serving time.

Nutrients per serving:

Calories 194; Fat 8 gm.; Cholesterol 0; Sodium 335 mg.;
Food exchange value: 1 lean meat, 1 vegetable, 1 fat, 1 bread/starch

"I think that life is not too long,
And therefore I determine
That many people read a song
Who will not read a sermon."

-Winthrop Praed, Chant of the Brazen Head

Trumpets Sounding Melon and Shrimp Salad

8 servings — 1 cup each

2 lb. cooked shrimp
1 small cantaloupe, cut in balls
1 small honeydew melon, cut in balls
2 green onions, finely diced
4 ribs celery, diced

Dressing:
2 Tbsp. lemon juice
1 tsp. salt
1 1/2 tsp. curry powder
1 c. reduced-fat mayonnaise
Optional garnish: 2 Tbsp. chopped peanuts

Combine salad ingredients in a large salad bowl. In a small mixing bowl, combine ingredients for the dressing. Mix dressing with salad just before serving. Garnish with chopped peanuts if desired. Serve with hot breadsticks or a white dinner roll.

Nutrients per serving (without peanuts):
*Calories 130; Fat 6 gm; Cholesterol 43 mg; Sodium 297 mg;
Food exchange value: 1 fruit, 1 lean meat, 1/2 fat*

"Wherever you go, whatever you do—
always make friends with the cook."

- John Ratzenberger

Magic Ingredient
Taco Salad

8 servings — 3 cups each

1 lb. lean ground beef
1/2 c. raisins
1 envelope taco seasoning mix
1 c. water
8 oz. baked corn chips
1 head lettuce, cleaned and shredded
15-oz. can red kidney beans, drained and rinsed
2 fresh tomatoes, chopped
3 green onions, chopped
4 oz. reduced-fat cheddar cheese, shredded
1 c. picante sauce

In a medium skillet, cook and crumble ground beef over medium heat until it's no longer pink; drain well. Return drained meat to the skillet. Stir in raisins, taco mix, and water. Bring to a boil, then simmer uncovered for 10 minutes.

Meanwhile, assemble the salads on 8 chilled plates, layering chips and lettuce first. Spoon the hot seasoned beef over the lettuce. Add beans, tomatoes, onions, cheese, and picante sauce. Serve immediately.

Nutrients per serving:

Calories 233; Fat 5 gm; Cholesterol 40 mg; Sodium 316 mg;
Food exchange value: 1 bread/starch, 2 vegetables, 2 lean meat

"Do you know that we shall judge the angels?"

-I Corinthians 6:3

Green Goddess Tuna Salad

8 servings — 3/4 cup each

1/2 c. Green Goddess salad dressing
2 c. cooked rice
1/4 c. raisins
2 green onions, chopped fine
2 6-oz. cans water-packed tuna, drained well
3 stalks celery, sliced thin
1 small red pepper, chopped
1/4 c. chopped fresh parsley
4-oz. can chopped pimientos, drained

Mix all ingredients together in a medium salad bowl, and chill for at least an hour before serving.

Nutrients per serving:

Calories 182; Fat 7 gm; Cholesterol 9 mg; Sodium 270 mg; Food exchange value: 1 vegetable, 1 lean meat, 1 bread/starch, 1/2 fat

"In Heaven a spirit doth dwell
'Whose heart-strings are a lute. . . .'"

-Edgar Allen Poe, Israfel

Cherubic Chicken
Pasta Salad

8 servings — 1 1/2 cups each

1-lb. package rotelle pasta
15-oz. can sliced, stewed tomatoes, drained
1 medium yellow crookneck squash, diced
2 c. cubed, cooked chicken or turkey
1/2 c. reduced-fat Italian dressing
1 green bell pepper, sliced into strips
Romaine lettuce
Cilantro

Prepare rotelle according to package directions. Rinse in cold water, cover, and refrigerate. In a large bowl, combine tomatoes, squash, chicken, dressing, and bell pepper. Cover and refrigerate 1 hour to blend flavors.

At least an hour before serving, combine noodles and chicken mixture. Toss gently. Return to the refrigerator for at least another hour.

Line 8 plates with lettuce. Serve 1 1/2-cup servings of the pasta salad onto the lettuce. Top with freshly snipped cilantro.

Nutrients per serving:

*Calories 348; Fat 7 gm.; Cholesterol 49 mg.; Sodium 233 mg.;
Food exchange value: 3 bread/starch, 1 vegetable, 1 1/2 fat*

"A baby is an angel whose
wings decrease as his legs increase."

-French proverb

Sublime Shrimp Salad

4 servings — 2 cups each

8 oz. angel hair pasta
1 c. zucchini, cubed
1/2 medium yellow bell pepper, chopped
4 green onions, sliced
12 oz. frozen, cooked shrimp, thawed
1/4 c. black olives, chopped
1/2 c. reduced-calorie Dijon vinaigrette
   salad dressing
1 c. quartered cherry tomatoes
Romaine lettuce

Break raw angel hair pasta into thirds. Cook as directed on package; drain. Rinse with cold water. In a large bowl, combine pasta, zucchini, bell pepper, onions, shrimp, and black olives. Pour dressing over salad; toss gently to coat. Cover and refrigerate 2 hours to allow flavors to blend.

When ready to serve, add tomatoes to salad. Gently toss again and serve on lettuce leaves.

Nutrients per serving:

Calories 145; Fat 2 gm; Cholesterol 51 mg; Sodium 113 mg;
Food exchange value: 1 bread/starch, 1 vegetable, 1 lean meat

"And yet, as angels in some brighter dreams
Call to the soul when man doth sleep,
so some strange thoughts transcend our
wonted themes, and into glory peep."

-Henry Vaughan, They Are All Gone

Zidkiel's Fruitful Chicken Salad

8 servings—2/3 cup each

1/2 c. nonfat mayonnaise
1/2 c. nonfat sour cream
1 Tbsp. prepared Dijon-style mustard
1/2 tsp. crushed fennel seeds
4 c. cubed, cooked chicken or turkey breast
15-oz. can pineapple chunks, drained
11-oz. can mandarin oranges, drained
1 c. chopped celery
1/2 c. chopped yellow bell pepper
1/4 c. sliced black olives
1 Tbsp. grated onion
Lettuce

In a large bowl, blend mayonnaise, sour cream, mustard, and fennel. Add chicken, pineapple, oranges, celery, bell pepper, olives, and onion. Toss gently to coat. Cover and chill 3 to 4 hours.

Serve in lettuce-lined bowls.

Nutrients per serving:
Calories 173; Fat 2 gm; Cholesterol 324 mg; Sodium 315 mg;
Food exchange value: 2 lean meat, 1 fruit

Hungry Angel Potato Soup

8 servings—6 ounces each

1 tsp. vegetable oil
1 small onion, chopped
3 Tbsp. flour
1 1/4 tsp. dry mustard
1/4 tsp. minced garlic
1/4 tsp. paprika
3 c. skim milk
2 tsp. chicken bouillon granules
2 tsp. Worcestershire sauce
4 stalks celery, sliced thin
16-oz. can sliced potatoes, drained
4 oz. reduced-fat Cheddar cheese, shredded
Garnish: 2 strips bacon, broiled and crumbled

Combine oil and onion in a large microwave-safe glass bowl.
Microwave for 1 minute on high power, then stir and microwave
again for 3 minutes. Add flour, dry mustard, garlic, and paprika.
Mix well. Use a whisk to stir in milk. Add bouillon, Worcestershire
sauce, and celery. Microwave uncovered for 10 minutes.

Stir in potatoes and cheese, and microwave again for 8 minutes or until bubbly. Ladle into soup cups, and garnish with crumbled bacon.

Nutrients per serving:
Calories 163; Fat 4 gm; Cholesterol 13 mg; Sodium 394 mg
(to reduce sodium, use low-sodium bouillon)
Food exchange value: 1 skim milk, 1/2 fat, 1/2 bread/starch

"His angel guards those who have reverence for the Lord and rescues them from danger."

-Psalms 34:7

"Look homeward, Angel, now,
and melt with ruth."

-John Milton, Lycidas

Busy Angel
Beef Barley Soup

8 servings—1 1/2 cups each

1 lb. round steak, finely diced
6 c. water
16-oz. can chunky tomatoes
1 large onion, diced
2 tsp. instant beef bouillon granules
2 large carrots, sliced thin
4 stalks celery, sliced thin
1/2 c. pearl barley
1/4 c. fresh parsley, minced
1/2 tsp. salt (optional)
1/2 tsp. pepper
2 tsp. basil
1 tsp. Worcestershire sauce

Combine all ingredients in a slow cooker. Cook on high for 4 hours or until meat is done to desired tenderness.

Nutrients per serving:

Calories 140; Fat 3 gm; Cholesterol 30 mg;
Sodium 368 mg with salt, 235 mg without salt;
Food exchange value: 1 vegetable, 1/2 bread/starch, 1 1/2 lean meat

"Bless the Lord, ye his angels,
that excel in strength, that do his
commandments, hearkening unto
the voice of his word."

-Psalms 103:20

Soulful Chicken Soup

8 servings — 1 1/2 cups each

8 c. no-added-salt chicken broth
Juice of 1 large lemon
2 carrots, shredded
1 medium onion, chopped
2 stalks celery, chopped
1/2 tsp. white pepper
2 Tbsp. softened margarine
1/4 c. flour
1 egg or 1/4 c. liquid egg substitute
1 c. cooked rice or 1/2 c. dry instant rice
2 c. diced cooked chicken

Combine first 6 ingredients in a Dutch oven. Bring to a boil, then reduce heat, and simmer 15 minutes. In a small mixing bowl, blend softened margarine and flour until smooth. Stir egg into the margarine and flour. Spoon 1/2 cup of the hot broth into the flour mixture, and stir until smooth. Transfer the flour and broth mixture into the Dutch oven a little at a time, whisking well after each addition. Stir in rice and chicken. Heat through, and serve.

Nutrients per serving:

Calories 153; Fat 4 gm; Cholesterol 63 mg with egg, 36 mg with egg substitute; Sodium 47 mg; Food exchange value: 2 lean meat, 2 vegetable

"God revealed to these prophets
that their work was not for their own benefit,
but for yours, as they spoke about those things
which you have now heard from the messen-
gers who announced the Good News by the
power of the Holy Spirit sent from heaven.
These are things which even the angels
would like to understand."

- I Peter 1:12

Divine French Onion Soup

4 servings—1 1/2 cups each

2 Tbsp. margarine
4 medium onions, thinly sliced
2 tsp. all-purpose flour
1 tsp. sugar
2 tsp. dry mustard
3 c. reduced-sodium chicken broth
1/4 c. dry white wine
2 tsp. reduced-sodium soy sauce
1 c. seasoned croutons
1/4 c. reduced-fat grated Parmesan cheese
1/2 c. reduced-fat mozzarella cheese

Place margarine in a 3-quart casserole, and microwave at full power for 15 seconds or until melted. Stir in onions, and microwave at full power for 7 to 10 minutes, stirring every 5 minutes, until onions are soft. Add flour, sugar, and mustard; mix well. Stir in broth, wine, and soy sauce. Cook at full power for 9 to 10 minutes, stirring every 2 minutes, until soup is thickened and bubbly.

Ladle soup into 4 bowls. Top soup with croutons, Parmesan cheese, and mozzarella cheese. Return bowls to microwave at full power for 2 1/2 minutes or until cheese melts.

Nutrients per serving:
Calories 204; Fat 9 gm; Cholesterol 8 mg; Sodium 343 mg;
Food exchange value: 1 bread/starch, 2 vegetable, 1 1/2 fat

"If men were angels,
no government would be necessary."

-James Madison

Egg Drop From Heaven Soup

4 servings — 1 cup each

3 c. (2 cans) reduced-sodium chicken broth
1 Tbsp. cornstarch
1 Tbsp. dry sherry
2 tsp. reduced-sodium soy sauce
1/2 tsp. poultry seasoning
1/2 c. cooked chicken or turkey breast, cut into thin
   strips
1/2 c. snow peas
3 green onions and tops, sliced
2 eggs, beaten

Combine 1/4 cup chicken broth and cornstarch in a measuring cup. Stir until smooth. In a medium saucepan, combine cornstarch mixture, remaining chicken broth, sherry, soy sauce, poultry seasoning, chicken breast, peas, and onions. Cook over high heat until boiling, stirring occasionally. Reduce heat to low.

With a fork, stir broth in a swirling motion in one direction. Remove the fork, and slowly pour eggs into the swirling broth. Stir just until eggs are set in long strands. Serve immediately.

Nutrients per serving:
Calories 109; Fat 3 gm; Cholesterol 124 mg; Sodium 220 mg;
Food exchange value: 2 vegetable, 1 lean meat

Golden Cauliflower Soup

6 servings — 1 1/2 cups each

1 medium head cauliflower,
   separated into florets (about 4 cups)
2 c. water, separated
1/2 c. chopped onion
2 Tbsp. margarine
1/3 to 1/2 c. all-purpose flour
2 c. evaporated skim milk
1 Tbsp. reduced-sodium beef
   bouillon granules
1/2 c. shredded reduced-fat
   mozzarella cheese
1/8 tsp. ground allspice
Garnish: fresh cilantro (Italian parsley)
   or paprika

In a medium saucepan, cook cauliflower in 1 cup of water until tender. Reserve 1 cup of florets. Blend remaining cauliflower and cooking liquid in a blender or food processor, then set aside.

In a large heavy saucepan, cook onion in margarine until tender; stir in flour. Gradually add remaining 1 cup water, milk, and bouillon. Cook and stir until well blended and slightly thickened. Add cheese, pureed cauliflower, reserved florets, and allspice. Cook and stir until cheese melts and mixture is hot. Do not boil.

Garnish each serving with snipped cilantro or a dash of ground paprika.

Nutrients per serving:

Calories 191; Fat 6 gm; Cholesterol 8 mg; Sodium 144 mg;
Food exchange value: 1 skim milk, 1 vegetable, 1 bread/starch

City of Angels
Corn Bisque

6 servings — 1 cup each

2 c. fresh corn or frozen corn, thawed and drained
2 c. reduced-sodium chicken broth, defatted
2 Tbsp. margarine
1/4 c. chopped green onion
3 Tbsp. all-purpose flour
1/2 tsp. celery salt
1/4 tsp. chili powder
1 c. skim milk
2 Tbsp. chopped canned chilies
2 Tbsp. chopped pimiento
1/2 c. shredded reduced-fat mozzarella cheese
8 cherry tomatoes, halved
Garnish: snipped cilantro

In blender, combine 1 1/2 cups corn and 1/2 cup chicken broth. Process until smooth. Add remaining broth; set aside.

Place margarine in a deep 3-quart microwave casserole, and microwave on full power for 15 seconds, or until melted. Add green onion and remaining corn. Microwave on high for 2 1/2 to 3 minutes, or until vegetables are just tender.

Stir in flour, celery salt, and chili powder. Whisk in chicken broth mixture and milk; add chilies and pimiento. Microwave on high for 12 to 14 minutes, until mixture is thickened and bubbly, stirring every 3 to 4 minutes. Stir in cheese until melted. Microwave on high an additional 2 minutes or until soup is heated through.

Ladle soup into 6 bowls. Top each bowl with cherry tomato halves. Sprinkle with snipped cilantro if desired.

Nutrients per serving:

Calories 159; Fat 6 gm; Cholesterol 6 mg; Sodium 307 mg;
Food exchange value: 1 skim milk, 1 bread/starch

Hanael's Easy Friday Beer-Cheese Soup

4 servings — 1 cup each

2 Tbsp. margarine
3 Tbsp. all-purpose flour
1 Tbsp. onion powder
1/2 tsp. salt
1/2 tsp. garlic powder
3 c. skim milk
1 Tbsp. white wine Worcestershire sauce
1/2 c. light beer
1/2 c. shredded reduced-fat cheddar cheese (8 oz.)
1 Tbsp. Dijon-style mustard
Optional garnishes: Popcorn, snipped parsley, or
   chopped pimiento

Melt margarine in a medium saucepan. Add flour, and cook over medium heat, stirring constantly, for 2 minutes. Stir in onion powder, salt, garlic powder, milk, Worcestershire sauce, and beer. Blend thoroughly, and heat just to the boiling point. Reduce heat and simmer, stirring occasionally, for 10 minutes.

Stir in cheese and mustard. Simmer (do not boil), stirring constantly, an additional 5 minutes or until cheese melts. Garnish with freshly popped popcorn, snipped parsley, or chopped pimiento.

Nutrients per serving:

Calories 190; Fat 8 gm; Cholesterol 11 mg; Sodium 516 mg;
Food exchange value: 1 skim milk, 1/2 bread/starch, 1 fat

"The guardian angels of life sometimes fly
so high as to be beyond our sight,
but they are always looking down upon us."

-Jean Paul Richter

Salvation Soup

If your angel has an illness,
this remedy is ready in no time at all.
8 servings — 1 cup each

1 lb. lean ground beef
6 c. water
24-oz. can chunky tomatoes
2 Tbsp. dried onion flakes
1 1/2 tsp. dill weed
1 1/2 tsp. basil
1 tsp. garlic powder
3/4 tsp. thyme
1/4 tsp. black pepper
1 bay leaf
2 large raw potatoes, peeled and diced
1 c. chopped green cabbage
1 green pepper, diced
4 carrots, peeled and sliced thin
10-oz. pkg. frozen corn
9-oz. pkg. frozen cut green beans

Brown ground beef in a large Dutch oven, then drain fat. Add all remaining ingredients. Bring mixture to a boil, then reduce heat, uncover, and simmer for 30 minutes.

Nutrients per serving:

*Calories 154; Fat 2 gm; Cholesterol 30 mg; Sodium 178 mg;
Food exchange value: 1 vegetable, 1 bread/starch, 1 lean meat*

"It snows because angels are
having pillow fights!"

-Common angel legend

Soulful Cucumber Soup

8 servings — 3/4 cup each

    3 large cucumbers
    1 small onion, chopped fine
    1 Tbsp. margarine
    1 Tbsp. flour
    13-oz. can chicken broth
    1/2 tsp. salt
    8 oz. nonfat sour cream
    3 Tbsp. lemon juice
    Garnish: dill weed

Slice cucumbers, and sauté with onion in margarine for 1 to 2 minutes, just until soft. In a shaker container, combine flour and chicken broth. Stir slowly into the vegetables, and simmer for 15 minutes.

Transfer mixture to a blender, add salt, and process just until vegetables are finely diced. Use a wire whisk to fold in sour cream and lemon juice, and chill until serving time. Garnish soup with dill weed.

Nutrients per serving:
Calories 44; Fat 2 gm; Cholesterol 1 mg; Sodium 161 mg;
Food exchange value: 1 vegetable, 1/2 fat

"Sleep, my child, and peace attend thee
All through the night
Guardian angels God will send thee
All through the night."

–Sir Harold Boulton, All Through the Night

Archangel
Corn Relish Salad

8 servings — 2/3 cup each

1/2 c. sugar
1/4 c. canola oil
1/8 c. white wine vinegar
1/2 tsp. celery seed
1/4 tsp. whole mustard seed
2 c. fresh corn or frozen corn, thawed and drained
16-oz. can sauerkraut, pressed to remove
   excess liquid
1/2 c. diced green pepper
1/4 c. diced red pepper
8 green onion bulbs, chopped

In a medium bowl, combine sugar, oil, vinegar, celery, and mustard seed. Stir until sugar is dissolved. Add remaining ingredients; toss with a fork until well blended. Cover and refrigerate 4 hours or overnight.

Drain and stir before serving.

Nutrients per serving:
Calories 67; Fat 7 gm; Cholesterol 0; Sodium 419 mg;
Food exchange value: 1 bread/starch, 1/2 fruit, 1 fat

"And now it is an angel's song,
That makes the heavens be mute."

Samuel Taylor Coleridge,
The Rime of the Ancient Mariner

Harmonious Blended Fruit Salad

8 servings — 3/4 cup each

3 Tbsp. lemon juice
3 Tbsp. honey
1 tsp. oil
1/2 tsp. ginger
1 small can mandarin oranges, drained
4 fresh ripe pears, coarsely chopped
1 c. golden raisins
2 red apples (prefer Jonathans), coarsely chopped

Combine lemon juice, honey, oil, and ginger in a large bowl. Mix well. Add fruit, and toss to mix. Chill until serving time.

Nutrients per serving:
Calories 153; Fat 1 gm; Cholesterol 0; Sodium 4 mg;
Food exchange value: 2 1/2 fruit

"In Heaven a spirit doth dwell
'Whose heart-strings are a lute,'
None sing so wildly well
As the angel Israfel."

-Edgar Allen Poe, Israfel

Glorious Greek Salad

8 servings—2 to 3 cups each

2 Tbsp. olive oil
1/4 c. wine vinegar
1 tsp. salt (optional)
1 tsp. oregano
1 small head lettuce, washed and chopped
1 small cucumber, sliced thin
1 bunch radishes, washed and sliced thin
3 scallions, diced
2 fresh tomatoes, cut into thin wedges
12 green olives, sliced
4 oz. feta cheese, crumbled

Blend olive oil, vinegar, salt, and oregano in a shaker container until smooth. Combine vegetables and olives in a large salad bowl. Pour dressing over the salad; toss. Top with crumbled feta cheese.

Nutrients per serving:

Calories 83; Fat 6 gm; Cholesterol 13 mg; Sodium 461 mg with salt, 195 mg without salt; Food exchange value: 1 fat, 1 vegetable

"And flights of angels sing thee to thy rest!"

-William Shakespeare, Hamlet

Superior
Blue Cheese Dressing
8 servings — 1/4 cup each

4 oz. blue cheese
2 Tbsp. vinegar
3/4 c. nonfat sour cream
1/4 c. reduced-fat mayonnaise
2 tsp. chopped fresh chives
1/2 tsp. sugar
1/2 tsp. salt (optional)
1/2 tsp. Worcestershire sauce

Crumble the cheese into a plastic container with a tight-fitting lid
for refrigerator storage. Add all remaining ingredients, and mix well.
Chill until serving time. Use on your favorite green salads.

Nutrients per serving:

*Calories 101; Fat 6 gm.; Cholesterol 10 mg.; Sodium 419 mg with salt,
286 mg without salt; Food exchange value: 1/2 skim milk, 1 fat*

"Yet I am the necessary angel of earth,
Since, in my sight, you see the earth again. . . ."

Wallace Stevens,
Angel Surrounded by Paysans

We Adore Thee
Broccoli Salad

8 servings—3/4 cup each

1 large head broccoli, washed, stemmed, and diced
    into small pieces (or use a 1-lb. bag of prepared
    broccoli slaw from the produce section)
2 carrots, cleaned and grated
1 small red onion, finely chopped
1/4 c. raisins
4 strips bacon, diced, cooked crisp, and drained

Dressing:
1/2 c. reduced-fat mayonnaise
1/4 c. vinegar
2 Tbsp. sugar
1/2 tsp. salt
1/2 tsp. white pepper

Combine salad ingredients in a large salad bowl. In a small mixing
bowl, combine ingredients for dressing. Pour dressing over salad;
mix. Refrigerate until serving time.

Nutrients per serving:

Calories 120; Fat 5 gm; Cholesterol 2 mg; Sodium 312 mg;
Food exchange value: 2 vegetable, 1 fat, 1/2 fruit

"It thunders because angels are bowling!"

-Common angel legend

Seventh Heaven
Pea Salad
8 servings — 3/4 cup each

16-oz. pkg. frozen peas, thawed and drained
2 ribs celery, chopped
1/4 c. chopped peanuts
1/2 small red onion, chopped fine
4 strips bacon, diced, cooked crisp, and drained

Dressing:
1/3 c. reduced-fat mayonnaise
2 Tbsp. reduced-fat Italian salad dressing

Combine ingredients for salad in a salad bowl. Measure mayonnaise
in a glass cup measure and fold in Italian dressing. Pour over peas,
and gently mix to blend. Chill until serving time.

Nutrients per serving:
*Calories 130; Fat 5 gm; Cholesterol 1 mg; Sodium 127 mg;
Food exchange value: 1 bread/starch, 1 fat*

"Look how the floor of heaven
Is thick inlaid with patterns of bright gold.
There's not the smallest orb
which thou behold'st.
But in his motion like an angel sings,
Still quiring to the young-eyed cherubims."

-William Shakespeare, The Merchant of Venice

Kingdom Come
Coleslaw Soufflé

8 servings — 1 cup each

1 pkg. sugar-free or regular lemon gelatin
1 c. boiling water
2 Tbsp. vinegar
1/4 tsp. salt
1/4 tsp. pepper
1/2 c. cold water
1/3 c. reduced-fat mayonnaise
1-lb. bag shredded cabbage and carrots
1 green pepper, finely diced
1/4 c. diced onion
1/4 tsp. celery seed

In a small mixing bowl, pour boiling water over gelatin. Stir briskly to dissolve gelatin. Add vinegar, salt, pepper, and cold water, and chill for 15 minutes in the freezer.

With an electric mixer, beat the partially set gelatin mixture with the mayonnaise. Fold in vegetables and celery seed, and transfer to a salad bowl. Chill for at least 2 hours.

Nutrients per serving (using sugar-free gelatin):
Calories 46; Fat 3 gm; Cholesterol 0; Sodium 147 mg;
Food exchange value: 1 vegetable, 1/2 fat

Dolphins are known as "angels of the sea."

Melonious Salad
6 servings — 1/2 cup each

1 c. cantaloupe, cubed
1 c. honeydew melon, cubed
1/2 c. peeled, sliced kiwifruit
1/2 c. sliced fresh strawberries

Lemon-Ginger Dressing:
1/2 c. undiluted lemonade concentrate
1/2 tsp. dried ground ginger
1 Tbsp. vegetable oil

Combine fruit in a medium serving bowl. Set aside. In a small bowl, mix together lemonade, ginger, and oil. Blend well. Pour over fruit, and toss lightly to coat. Refrigerate until ready to serve.

Nutrients per serving:

Calories 94; Fat 3 gm; Cholesterol 0; Sodium 11 mg;
Food exchange value: 1 fruit, 1/2 fat

Entrees

"For when the dead rise to life, they will be like the angels in heaven and will not marry."

-Matthew 22:30

Hamburgers
With a Halo

4 servings — 3 ounces each

1 lb. lean ground beef, formed into 4 patties
1/2 c. soft cheddar cheese food (such as Kraft
    Spreadery®)
1 Tbsp. prepared yellow mustard
1 tsp. Worcestershire sauce

Grill or broil hamburgers until desired doneness. Soften cheese to
room temperature. In a small mixing bowl, combine soft cheese with
mustard and Worcestershire sauce. Put hamburgers on a serving
platter. Make a large halo on each hamburger with the cheese mixture. Serve with whole grain buns or light rye bread.

Nutrients per serving:

Calories 275; Fat 16 gm; Cholesterol 94 mg; Sodium 352 mg;
Food exchange value: 4 lean meat, 1/2 skim milk

"In 1512, Raphael completed the
Sistine Madonna. . . . Two naked infants with
colored wings and tangled hair lean on a small
painted pedestal and glance mischievously
at the figure of St. Barbara."

—James Underhill, Angels

Messenger's
Tuna Puffs
4 servings — 2 puffs each

2 5-oz. cans tuna packed in water, drained well
2 oz. reduced-fat cheddar cheese, grated
1/3 c. reduced-fat mayonnaise
1/4 c. chopped onion
1/4 c. chopped celery
2 drops Tabasco sauce
4 whole-grain hamburger rolls, cut in half
Optional garnish: green onion tops

Preheat oven to 350°. Mix the first 6 ingredients in a medium mixing bowl. Mound the tuna mixture on halved rolls, and place on a baking sheet. Bake for 8 to 12 minutes or until browned. Garnish the top of the puffs with minced green onion tops.

Nutrients per serving:
Calories 287; Fat 10 gm; Cholesterol 6 mg; Sodium 671 mg;
(to reduce sodium, use low-sodium tuna)
Food exchange value: 2 lean meat, 2 bread/starch, 1/2 fat

"No one can deny how great is
the secret of our religion: He appeared in
human form, was shown to be right by the
spirit and was seen by angels. He was preached
among the nations, was believed in throughout
the world and was taken up to heaven."

—I Timothy 3:16

Chicken After Church

8 servings—1 chicken breast and 3/4 cup rice each

Vegetable oil cooking spray
2 c. brown rice, dry
13-oz. can reduced-fat cream of mushroom soup
13-oz. can reduced-fat cream of chicken soup
2 Tbsp. white wine Worcestershire sauce
1 1/2 c. water
8 boneless, skinless chicken breast halves
7-oz. can sliced mushrooms, drained well

Assemble on Saturday and refrigerate:

Spray a 9" x 13" baking pan with cooking spray. Pour the dry brown rice into the pan, and spread evenly. In a small mixing bowl, combine soups, Worcestershire sauce, and water. Stir until smooth. Pour the soup over the rice. Lay chicken breasts on top of the soup. Sprinkle with sliced mushrooms. Cover.

On Sunday morning, preheat oven to 300°. Place the pan in the oven, and bake for 2 hours while you are gone to church. Serve with breadsticks and a dark green leafy salad.

Nutrients per serving:
Calories 236; Fat 4 gm; Cholesterol 74 mg; Sodium 593 mg;
(to reduce sodium, use low-sodium soup)
Food exchange value: 3 lean meat, 1 bread/starch

From Meat Loaf to Eternity

8 servings—2 to 3 ounces each

1 lb. 95% lean ground beef
1/2 lb. ground pork
1/2 c. chopped green pepper
2 egg whites
1 tsp. basil
1/2 tsp. black pepper
1/2 c. ketchup

Glaze:
1/4 c. brown sugar
1/4 c. spicy ketchup
1/2 tsp. nutmeg

Preheat oven to 350°. In a medium mixing bowl, combine ingredients for the meat loaf. Press the mixture into a loaf pan, and bake for 70 to 80 minutes.

Blend glaze ingredients in a small bowl, and spread over the loaf during the last 20 minutes of baking.

Note: If meat loaf is a family favorite, consider purchasing a perforated meat loaf pan set, which allows fat to drain from the first pan into the second pan.

Nutrients per serving:
Calories 165; Fat 4 gm; Cholesterol 45 mg; Sodium 301 mg;
Food exchange value: 2 lean meat, 1 fruit

"When a raindrop falls on your nose, you've
just been kissed by an angel."

-Common angel legend

"Music is well said to be the speech of angels."

-Thomas Carlyle, The Opera

Lyrical Beef Kabobs
4 servings — 1 skewer each

1 lb. boneless chuck
2 Tbsp. lemon juice
1 Tbsp. water
2 Tbsp. Dijon-style mustard
1 Tbsp. red cooking wine
1 medium zucchini
1/2 medium red bell pepper
8 large mushrooms
1/2 tsp. dried oregano
1/4 tsp. black pepper

Cut beef into 1-inch pieces. In a large bowl, whisk together lemon juice, water, mustard, and cooking wine. Add beef. Cover and marinate at least 2 hours or overnight.

Slice unpared zucchini into 1-inch thick chunks. Cut bell pepper into 1-inch pieces. Add zucchini, bell pepper, mushrooms, oregano, and black pepper to beef, and toss to coat vegetables with marinade.

Alternately thread pieces of beef, zucchini, mushrooms, and bell pepper on four 12-inch skewers. Place kabobs on rack in the broiler pan so the surface of the meat is 3 to 4 inches from heat. Broil 9 to 12 minutes for rare to medium, turning occasionally. Serve with cooked brown or wild rice.

Nutrients per serving:
Calories 240; Fat 9 gm; Cholesterol 86 mg; Sodium 159 mg;
Food exchange value: 4 lean meat, 1 vegetable

"God does not trust his heavenly servants;
he finds fault even with his angels."

-Job 4:18

Curried Turkey Pita Proclaimer

6 servings—2 stuffed pita halves each

1 c. finely diced cooked turkey
1/2 c. finely chopped apple
1/4 c. raisins
2 Tbsp. chopped celery
2 Tbsp. chopped green onion
2 Tbsp. chopped unsalted peanuts
2 Tbsp. reduced calorie mayonnaise
2 Tbsp. plain nonfat yogurt
1 tsp. curry powder
6 pita bread, sliced crosswise

In a medium bowl, combine turkey, apple, raisins, celery, green onion, and peanuts. Set aside. In a small bowl, mix together mayonnaise, yogurt, and curry powder. Blend well. Stir mayonnaise sauce into turkey mixture. Toss lightly. Spoon into pita bread halves.

Place on a paper-towel-lined plate. Microwave at full power for 2 1/2 to 3 minutes, or until filling is heated through, turning plate midway through the warming process.

Nutrients per serving:
Calories 240; Fat 3 gm; Cholesterol 13 mg; Sodium 370 mg;
Food exchange value: 1 lean meat, 2 bread/starch, 1/2 fruit

Flying Chicken Breasts Florentine

4 servings — 1 breast each

4 skinless, boneless chicken breasts
   (about 1 lb.)
4 thin slices Swiss cheese
10-oz. package frozen chopped spinach,
   thawed and well drained
14 1/2-oz. can reduced-sodium chicken broth
2 Tbsp. cornstarch
4 green onions, chopped (including tops)
1/4 tsp. dried thyme
1/4 tsp. dried marjoram

With the flat side of a meat mallet, pound chicken to 1/4-inch thickness. Place a slice of Swiss cheese and 1/4 of the spinach on each chicken piece. Roll up chicken from the short end, in jelly-roll fashion. Secure with wooden toothpicks. Place chicken, seam side down, in an 8" x 12" microwave-safe baking dish. Cover with vented plastic wrap, and microwave on high for 5 minutes.

Combine 1/4 cup chicken broth with cornstarch in a measuring cup. Stir until smooth. In a small saucepan, stir together remaining chicken broth, green onions, thyme, and marjoram. Pour in cornstarch mixture, and bring to a rolling boil. Continue to heat until sauce is thickened. Pour over chicken. Cover chicken again with vented plastic wrap. Heat in the microwave on high for an additional 10 minutes, or until chicken is fork tender, rotating dish once during cooking. Let stand, covered, for 5 minutes before serving.

Nutrients per serving:

Calories 258; Fat 7 gm; Cholesterol 86 mg; Sodium 182 mg;
Food exchange value: 4 lean meat, 1 vegetable

"Angels from the realms of glory,
wing your flight o'er all the earth;
Ye who sang creation's story,
now proclaim Messiah's birth."

-James Montgomery,
Angels From the Realms of Glory

Eastern Angel Tacos

4 servings — 1 taco each

1 lb. ground turkey
1/4 c. chopped green onion
1/4 c. chopped water chestnuts
2 Tbsp. cornstarch
2 Tbsp. reduced-sodium soy sauce, chilled
1 Tbsp. vinegar
1/2 tsp. dry mustard
1/2 tsp. dry ginger
1/8 tsp. five-spice powder
1/2 tsp. reduced-sodium beef bouillon granules
1/3 c. water
4 large crisp iceberg lettuce leaves
3-oz. can chow mein noodles
Reduced-sodium soy sauce
Plain nonfat yogurt

Crumble ground turkey in a 2-quart casserole. Add green onion. Cover with waxed paper, and microwave on full power for 5 minutes or until meat is browned, stirring twice. Pour off juices. Add water chestnuts to ground turkey.

In a small bowl, combine cornstarch, soy sauce, and vinegar. Stir in dry mustard, ginger, and five-spice powder. Blend until smooth. Spoon sauce over turkey mixture; stir well. Add bouillon granules and water, stirring until well mixed. Cover and microwave at full power for 3 minutes or until mixture is thickened and bubbly, stirring once.

To serve, place a lettuce leaf on each plate. Spoon some of the turkey mixture onto the center of the lettuce. Sprinkle with chow mein noodles. Fold up envelope-style to eat. Serve with additional soy sauce and yogurt.

Nutrients per serving:

Calories 250; Fat 3 gm; Cholesterol 61 mg; Sodium 309 mg;
Food exchange value: 3 lean meat, 1 bread/starch

Heavenly Halibut
With Sherry Sauce

4 servings — 6 ounces each

Vegetable oil cooking spray
1 1/2 lbs. fresh halibut, cut 1-inch thick, or frozen
    halibut, thawed and drained
1 Tbsp. olive oil
Pepper
1 medium white onion, coarsely chopped
1/2 c. sliced fresh mushrooms
1 Tbsp. no-salt seasoning, such as "Pleasoning"
1 Tbsp. margarine
4 tsp. flour
1/3 c. nonfat sour cream
1/2 c. reduced-sodium chicken broth, defatted
1 Tbsp. cooking sherry
Garnish: parsley

Spray the rack of a broiler pan with cooking spray. Place the fish on
the rack. Brush lightly with half of the olive oil, and sprinkle with
pepper. Broil 4 inches from heat for 5 minutes. Turn fish over, brush
with remaining olive oil, and broil an additional 5 minutes, or until
fish flakes easily when pierced with a fork.

In a small saucepan, cook onions, no-salt seasoning, and mushrooms in margarine until tender. Add flour and sour cream. Stir in broth. Cook until bubbly. Stir in sherry. Cook and stir 1 minute more.

Place fish on a serving plate. Ladle sauce over fish. Garnish with snipped parsley if desired.

Nutrients per serving:

Calories 289; Fat 10 gm; Cholesterol 53 mg; Sodium 152 mg; Food exchange value: 4 lean meat, 1 vegetable, 1/2 bread/starch

"Angels we have heard on high,
sweetly singing o'er the plains,
and the mountains in reply
echoing their joyous strains."

-From the French carol Crown of Jesus

Creole Scallop Celebration

4 servings — 1/2 cup scallops each

12 oz. fresh scallops (approx. 2 cups)
1/2 c. milk (optional*)
1/4 c. chopped yellow onion
1/2 c. chopped yellow bell pepper
1/2 c. cubed, unpared zucchini
2 cloves garlic, minced
2 Tbsp. margarine
16-oz. can sliced stewed tomatoes, undrained
1/8 - 1/4 tsp. cayenne pepper
1 bay leaf
4 oz. uncooked angel hair pasta
1 Tbsp. cornstarch
2 Tbsp. cold water
1/4 c. water

In a large skillet, cook onion, bell pepper, zucchini, garlic, and margarine until vegetables are tender, but not browned. Stir in tomatoes, cayenne pepper, and bay leaf. Bring to a boil. Cover, reduce heat, and simmer for 15 minutes, stirring occasionally.

While sauce is simmering, prepare pasta according to package directions.

Stir together cornstarch and cold water. Add cornstarch mixture, 1/4 cup water, and scallops to tomato mixture. Cook and stir until sauce is thickened and bubbly, and scallops have turned opaque. Remove bay leaf, and toss sauce with hot pasta.

*If you prefer a less fishy taste, place scallops in a medium bowl with 1/2 c. milk, cover, and refrigerate for 10 to 15 minutes. Pour into a colander, rinse, and drain.

Nutrients per serving:
Calories 255; Fat 7 gm; Cholesterol 15 mg; Sodium 453 mg;
Food exchange value: 2 bread/starch

"But when God was about to send his
first-born son into the world, he said,
'All of God's angels must worship him.'"

-Hebrews 1:6

October 2 is the feast day of guardian angels
and time to say thanks to an angel for all
the help you've been given.

Pearly Gates
Turkey Biscuit Bake

5 servings — 1 wedge each

Vegetable oil cooking spray
1 lb. ground turkey
1 Tbsp. olive oil
2 Tbsp. Italian seasoning
1 c. no-salt-added stewed tomatoes, drained
1/2 tsp. garlic powder
8 oz. fresh mushrooms, cleaned and sliced
1/2 tsp. salt
3/4 c. shredded part-skim mozzarella cheese
1 can buttermilk refrigerator biscuits (10 biscuits)

Spray a 1 1/2-quart round casserole with cooking spray.

In a large skillet, brown ground turkey in olive oil. Add Italian seasoning, tomatoes, garlic powder, mushrooms, and salt. Simmer, covered, for 5 minutes. Spoon meat mixture into prepared casserole. Sprinkle with mozzarella cheese. Open biscuits and separate. Place biscuits, sides touching, on top of the cheese in the casserole. Bake as directed on biscuit package, until biscuits are golden brown. Let stand 5 minutes before serving. Cut into 5 wedges.

Nutrients per serving:

*Calories 292; Fat 9 gm.; Cholesterol 58 mg.; Sodium 465 mg.;
Food exchange value: 1 bread/starch, 1 vegetable, 3 1/2 lean meat*

"Every visible thing in this world is put
in the charge of an angel."

-St. Augustine

Italian Steaks With Angel Hair Pasta

4 servings—2 cups each

4 oz. angel hair pasta, cooked and drained
1 lb. lean beef round tip steaks
2 cloves garlic, crushed
2 tsp. olive oil, separated
2 c. broccoli florets
1/8 c. water
1 c. cherry tomato halves
1/4 c. reduced-fat Italian salad dressing
2 Tbsp. grated Parmesan cheese

Cut steaks crosswise into 1-inch strips. Cut strips crosswise in half. In a large skillet, heat half of the garlic and 1 teaspoon olive oil over medium heat for 1 minute. Add half of the beef strips. Stir-fry 1 to 2 minutes. Using a slotted spoon, remove beef to a bowl. Cover and keep warm. Repeat with remaining garlic, oil, and beef strips.

Add broccoli and water to the same skillet. Steam for 5 minutes, until florets are just tender. Return beef to the skillet, along with tomato halves and dressing. Cook an additional 2 to 3 minutes, until heated through. Serve beef over hot pasta, and top with Parmesan cheese.

Nutrients per serving:

Calories 337; Fat 11 gm; Cholesterol 77 mg; Sodium 171 mg;
Food exchange value: 1 1/2 bread/starch, 2 vegetable, 3 lean meat

Michael's Manicotti

8 servings — 1 shell each

8 manicotti shells
Vegetable oil cooking spray
1 egg
1 c. nonfat ricotta cheese
2 6-oz. cans water-packed tuna, drained and flaked
1/2 c. herb-seasoned stuffing mix, dry
1/4 c. chopped black olives
1/4 c. reduced-fat Parmesan cheese
2 Tbsp. fresh parsley (1 Tbsp. dried)
2 Tbsp. snipped cilantro
Garnish: snipped chives

Sauce:
2 Tbsp. margarine
1 c. diced yellow crookneck squash
1/2 c. diced onion
1/2 c. chopped red bell pepper
1/4 c. flour
1/2 tsp. salt
1 tsp. lemon pepper
1 3/4 c. evaporated skim milk

Cook and drain the manicotti shells according to package directions. While the shells are cooking, prepare the sauce. In a 1 1/2-quart microwave-safe casserole, combine margarine, squash, onion, and red pepper. Microwave at full power for 3 to 5 minutes, or until vegetables are just tender. Blend in flour, salt, and lemon pepper. Microwave at full power for 30 seconds. Whisk in evaporated milk. Microwave at full power 5 to 7 minutes or until mixture is thickened and bubbling, stirring every 2 minutes. Mixture should be thick and smooth. Spray a microwave-safe pie plate with cooking spray. Pour 1/3 of the sauce into the prepared pie plate. Set aside remaining sauce.

In a medium bowl, beat the egg. Stir in ricotta cheese, tuna, stuffing mix, olives, Parmesan cheese, parsley, and cilantro. Mix well.

Spoon 1/3 cup of the ricotta mixture into each manicotti shell. Place manicotti on the sauce in the pie plate, in spoke fashion with one end of each shell pointing to the center of the plate. Place any remaining ricotta cheese mixture between the manicotti "spokes." Pour the remaining sauce over the shells, coating all the pasta.

Cover the dish with vented plastic wrap, and microwave at 50 percent (medium) for 20 to 25 minutes or until heated through, giving dish a half-turn after 10 minutes. At end of cooking time, stir sauce, then spoon sauce back over pasta shells. Garnish with snipped chives if desired. Allow to stand 5 minutes before serving.

Nutrients per serving:
*Calories 277; Fat 6 gm; Cholesterol 38 mg; Sodium 417 mg;
Food exchange value: 2 bread/starch, 1 vegetable, 2 lean meat*

St. Peter's Pizza Casserole

10 servings — 1/10 of pan each

Vegetable oil cooking spray
1 lb. ground turkey
15-oz. can tomato sauce
6-oz. can tomato paste
1 c. chopped onion
1/2 c. chopped green pepper
8 oz. fresh mushrooms, sliced
2 cloves garlic, minced
1 Tbsp. dried oregano
1 Tbsp. dried thyme
1 Tbsp. dried basil
1/2 tsp. salt
1/2 c. skim milk
2 Tbsp. margarine, melted
1/2 c. egg substitute
1 1/4 c. flour
1 c. shredded reduced-fat mozzarella cheese

Spray a 9" x 13" pan with cooking spray. Preheat oven to 400°.

Brown ground turkey in a 12-inch skillet. Drain juices from turkey. Stir in tomato sauce and paste. Add onion, green pepper, mushrooms, garlic, herbs, and salt. Bring to a boil. Reduce heat and simmer, covered, 10 minutes.

In a small bowl, use a mixer at medium speed to beat together milk, margarine, and egg substitute for one minute. Add flour, and beat for an additional 2 minutes. Set aside.

Turn meat mixture into the prepared pan. Sprinkle with mozzarella cheese. Top cheese with flour mixture. Bake for 30 minutes, until puffed and golden. Let stand 5 minutes before serving. Cut into 10 servings.

Nutrients per serving:

Calories 202; Fat 5 gm; Cholesterol 21 mg; Sodium 514 mg; Food exchange value: 1 1/2 bread/starch, 1 vegetable, 1 lean meat

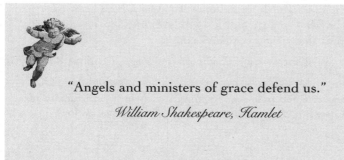

"Angels and ministers of grace defend us."

William Shakespeare, Hamlet

Pesto Shrimp
Over Angel Hair

4 servings—1 1/2 cups each

2 Tbsp. olive oil
2 cloves garlic, minced
3 Tbsp. dried basil
1/2 tsp. salt
1 tsp. oregano
2 medium tomatoes, chopped
8 oz. dry angel hair pasta
12 oz. cooked shrimp, peeled and deveined
2 Tbsp. crushed pine (pignoli) nuts

Heat olive oil in a medium skillet over medium-high heat. Add garlic, and simmer 1 minute. Stir in basil, salt, oregano, and tomatoes. Reduce heat to low, and simmer 5 minutes.

Cook the angel hair pasta according to package directions. Drain.

Return heat under the tomato mixture to medium-high, and stir in shrimp and crushed pine nuts, coating the shrimp with tomato mixture. Simmer 5 to 7 minutes, until shrimp is warmed and curling inward.

In a large bowl, combine hot pasta and shrimp mixture. Toss to coat, and serve.

Nutrients per serving:

Calories 265; Fat 9 gm; Cholesterol 70 mg; Sodium 341 mg;
Food exchange value: 2 bread/starch, 1 vegetable, 1 1/2 lean meat

"It is wonderful that every angel,
in whatever direction he turns his body
and face, sees the Lord in front of him."

-Emanuel Swedenborg,
The True Christian Religion

Golden Guardian
Lasagna Bordelaise

6 servings — 1/6 of dish each

Vegetable oil cooking spray
9 lasagna noodles (8 oz.), cooked and drained
2 medium yellow squash, sliced thin lengthwise
   (2 cups)
2 c. water
1/2 c. reduced-sodium chicken broth
1 Tbsp. cornstarch
1 tsp. olive oil
1 medium yellow onion, chopped
1 sweet yellow bell pepper, chopped
4 oz. mushrooms, sliced
1 tsp. garlic powder
1/2 tsp. dried thyme
1 tsp. dried basil
1 tsp. dried oregano
1/4 c. dry white wine
1/4 c. shredded reduced-fat mozzarella cheese
2/3 c. nonfat cottage cheese
1/4 c. grated Parmesan cheese

Spray an oven-safe 8" x 11 1/2" baking dish with cooking spray. Preheat oven to 375°.

In a medium saucepan, place squash in a steamer basket over 2 cups water. Bring water to a boil, and steam, covered, for 5 to 6 minutes, or until just tender. Remove squash from steamer, and shake off excess moisture.

In 1 cup measure, combine chicken broth and the cornstarch; stir until smooth. Set aside.

Heat the olive oil in a large skillet. Add onions, bell pepper, and mushrooms, stirring until lightly sautéed. Add garlic powder, thyme, basil, oregano, wine, and cornstarch mixture. Heat gently until mixture thickens and begins to bubble. Add squash; stir to coat.

In a small bowl, combine the mozzarella and cottage cheese, and set aside. In the prepared baking dish, layer 3 lasagna noodles, half the cheese mixture, then half the squash mixture. Repeat with one more layer, then top off with remaining 3 noodles. Sprinkle Parmesan cheese over the top layer of noodles.

Bake for 30 minutes, or until noodles start to brown at the edges. Cut into 6 servings.

Nutrients per serving:

Calories 244; Fat 5 gm; Cholesterol 9 mg; Sodium 101 mg;
Food exchange value: 1 skim milk, 1 vegetable, 1 bread/starch, 1 lean meat

Divine Lemon-Pepper Swordfish

4 servings — 1 swordfish steak each

4 6-oz. swordfish steaks,
    1/2-inch thick
Vegetable oil cooking spray

Marinade:
1/4 c. water
1/4 c. lemon juice
2 Tbsp. corn syrup
2 Tbsp. white vinegar
1 Tbsp. oil
2 tsp. minced onion
2 tsp. dill seed
1 Tbsp. freshly ground
    black pepper

Combine marinade ingredients in a medium bowl. Set aside.

Rinse swordfish steaks, and gently prick the top and bottom with a fork. Place steaks in a large casserole. Stir marinade, then pour over steaks. Cover and refrigerate 15 minutes.

Spray a broiler pan with cooking spray. Put steaks on the broiler pan. Brush with half the marinade, and place under the broiler approximately 4 inches from heat. Broil 4 minutes. Turn steaks over, brush with remaining marinade, and return to broiler for an additional 4 to 6 minutes, or until fish flakes easily with a fork.

Nutrients per serving:
Calories 264; Fat 10 gm; Cholesterol 66 mg; Sodium 164 mg;
Food exchange value: 5 lean meat

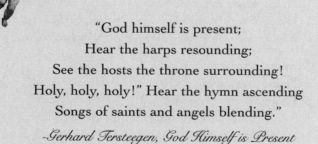

"God himself is present;
Hear the harps resounding;
See the hosts the throne surrounding!
Holy, holy, holy!" Hear the hymn ascending
Songs of saints and angels blending."

—Gerhard Tersteegen, God Himself is Present

Saintly
Stuffed Shells

8 servings—2 shells each

16 jumbo pasta shells
Vegetable oil cooking spray
1 lb. ground turkey sausage*
1/4 c. finely chopped green onion
4 oz. chopped fresh mushrooms, stems removed
1/2 c. fine dry seasoned bread crumbs*
2 Tbsp. snipped parsley
2 Tbsp. dry white wine
1 Tbsp. dried oregano
1 Tbsp. dried thyme
Garnish: snipped parsley and paprika (optional)

Mornay Sauce:
3 Tbsp. margarine
6 Tbsp. all-purpose flour
1 1/2 c. reduced-sodium chicken broth
1 1/2 c. skim milk
1/4 c. Parmesan cheese

Prepare shells according to package directions. Spray a microwave-safe 9" x 13" baking dish with cooking spray.

Crumble turkey sausage in a 1 1/2-quart casserole. Microwave at full power for 5 minutes, or until sausage is browned, stirring twice. Pour off juices, and pat dry with a paper towel. Stir in green onion, mushrooms, crumbs, parsley, wine, oregano, and thyme. Mix well. Spoon stuffing into cooked pasta shells, and place each shell, stuffing side up, into the prepared baking dish. Set aside.

Place the margarine in the same 1 1/2-quart casserole. Cover with waxed paper. Microwave margarine on high for 15 seconds or until melted. Stir in flour. Add chicken broth, milk, and Parmesan cheese; mix well. Microwave on high for 8 minutes, stirring every two minutes. Mixture should be thick and bubbly.

Pour Mornay sauce over stuffed shells, covering pasta completely. Cover the baking dish with vented plastic wrap, and microwave on high for 7 to 8 minutes, or until heated through, giving dish a half-turn after about 4 minutes. Spoon sauce over shells again before serving. Sprinkle with snipped parsley and paprika if desired.

Nutrients per serving:

*Calories 397; Fat 11 gm; Cholesterol 3 mg; Sodium 650 mg;
Food exchange value: 3 bread/starch, 2 lean meat, 1 fat*

*Turkey sausage and seasoned bread crumbs contribute most of the sodium. To reduce sodium, use plain dry bread crumbs.

Turkey Tetrazzini With Angel Hair

6 servings—1 1/2 cups each

4 slices turkey bacon
3 1/2 Tbsp. water
3/4 c. sliced fresh mushrooms
1/3 c. chopped onion
6 Tbsp. all-purpose flour
1/4 tsp. white pepper
1 1/2 c. reduced-sodium chicken broth, defatted
1 1/2 c. evaporated skim milk
3 Tbsp. cooking sherry
2 c. cubed cooked turkey breast
6 Tbsp. grated Parmesan cheese
10 oz. angel hair pasta, cooked and drained
Garnish: snipped parsley (optional)

Place bacon in a 12" x 7" baking dish with a microwave rack. Cover with a paper towel, and microwave at full power for 6 to 7 minutes, or until bacon is crisp. Drain grease from bacon, reserving 1 tablespoon. Crumble bacon, and set aside.

Remove rack from baking dish. Pour reserved bacon grease and water into baking dish. Add mushrooms and onions, and microwave on high for 4 to 5 minutes, or until onion is tender, stirring once.

Stir in flour and pepper, and microwave on high for 30 seconds.
Add chicken broth and evaporated milk. Mix well. Microwave on
high for 9 to 10 minutes, until sauce is thickened and bubbly, stirring every two minutes. Add sherry to broth mixture. Stir in turkey
cubes, crumbled bacon, and Parmesan cheese.

Toss with angel hair pasta. Cover with vented plastic wrap, and
microwave on high for 13 to 15 minutes or until heated through,
stirring well after 7 minutes.

Stir before serving. Garnish with snipped parsley, if desired.

Nutrients per serving:
Calories 351; Fat 5 gm; Cholesterol 39 mg; Sodium 223 mg;
Food exchange value: 3 bread/starch, 2 lean meat

Heavenly Halibut Steaks with Cheese and Herbs

4 servings — 1 halibut steak each

Vegetable oil cooking spray
4 oz. nonfat cream cheese
1/2 tsp. garlic powder
1 tsp. oregano
1 tsp. basil
2 Tbsp. snipped chives, separated
2 Tbsp. prepared horseradish
4 6-oz. halibut steaks, about 1/2-inch thick
1/2 c. thinly sliced yellow squash

Spray a 12" x 7" microwave-safe baking dish with cooking spray. In a small bowl, whisk together cream cheese, garlic powder, oregano, basil, 1 tablespoon chives, and horseradish. Set aside.

Arrange halibut steaks in the prepared baking dish, placing larger pieces and thicker portions toward the outside of the dish. Spread cheese mixture on steaks. Cover with vented plastic wrap, and microwave at full power for 4 minutes. Give dish a half-turn, then continue cooking for 4 minutes, or until center of fish flakes when tested with a fork.

Place squash slices on steaks. Sprinkle with remaining snipped chives. Return to microwave, covered with vented plastic wrap, and cook on high for an additional 3 minutes. Let stand, covered, for 5 minutes before serving.

Nutrients per serving:

*Calories 232; Fat 7 gm; Cholesterol 66 mg; Sodium 150 mg;
Food exchange value: 4 lean meat*

"In this theater of man's life, it is reserved only for God and angels to be lookers-on."

-Pythagoras

One Dish Celestial Lamb Chop Dinner

4 servings — 1 lamb chop each with 1/3 cup vegetables

Vegetable oil cooking spray
6 small new potatoes, quartered
1 c. baby carrots
1/4 c. chopped green onion
1/2 tsp. dried oregano
1/2 tsp. dried basil
4 6-oz lamb loin chops, 1-inch thick
1 tsp. dry mustard
1/4 tsp. garlic powder
4 lemon slices, halved

Spray the bottom of a 12" x 7" microwave-safe baking dish with cooking spray. Layer new potatoes, baby carrots, and green onion in the dish. Sprinkle evenly with oregano and basil.

Trim all fat from lamb chops. Rub chops with mustard and garlic powder. Place chops on vegetables in the baking dish. Top each chop with 2 half-slices of lemon, rind edges touching, for a "winged" effect.

Cover and microwave at full power for 10 minutes. Give dish a half-turn, and return to microwave at 50 percent power for 20 to 25 minutes, or until vegetables and meat are tender. Let stand, covered, 3 minutes before serving.

Nutrients per serving:

Calories 277; Fat 8 gm; Cholesterol 95 mg; Sodium 90 mg;
Food exchange value: 1 bread/starch, 3 1/2 lean meat

"I looked over Jordan and what did I see
Comin' for to carry me home?
A band of angels, comin' after me,
Comin' for to carry me home."

-African-American spiritual
Swing Low, Sweet Chariot

"Angels from friendship gather half their joy."

-Edward Young

Bugler's Turkey Bulgur Bake

4 servings — 2/3 cup each

2 c. cubed, cooked turkey breast
16-oz. can sliced, stewed tomatoes, undrained
1 medium yellow squash, halved lengthwise
   and sliced
1/2 c. bulgur
1/2 c. chopped yellow onion
1/2 tsp. salt
1 tsp. dried summer savory
1/4 tsp. black pepper
1/4 tsp. cayenne pepper
4 Tbsp. Parmesan cheese

Preheat oven to 375°. Combine all ingredients except Parmesan cheese in a 1 1/2- to 2-quart casserole. Mix well. Cover and bake 45 to 50 minutes, until bulgur is tender. Sprinkle with Parmesan cheese, and serve.

Nutrients per serving:

Calories 217; Fat 4 gm; Cholesterol 44 mg; Sodium 777 mg
(to reduce sodium, use no-added-salt tomatoes and omit salt)
Food exchange value: 2 lean meat, 1 bread/starch, 1 vegetable

Shining Shrimp Creole

4 servings—1 1/2 cups each

2 Tbsp. olive oil
2 Tbsp. lemon juice
2 Tbsp. oregano
1 Tbsp. thyme
2 cloves garlic, crushed
3 drops Tabasco sauce
1 medium green pepper, cut into chunks
1 medium onion, sliced
15-oz. can sliced stewed tomatoes, undrained
1 lb. uncooked medium shrimp, peeled and
    deveined
2 cups hot cooked rice

Combine oil, lemon juice, oregano, thyme, garlic, and Tabasco in a medium skillet. Warm over medium-high heat. Add green pepper and onion. Cook for 3 to 5 minutes, until vegetables are tender.

Reduce heat to medium. Add tomatoes, and simmer, covered, for 15 minutes. Add shrimp, cover, and simmer an additional 5 to 7 minutes, until shrimp turns pink and ends of shrimp begin to curl inward.

To serve, place rice in a large serving bowl. Spread rice to form a circle around the sides of the bowl. Place shrimp mixture in the middle of the rice ring.

Nutrients per serving:

Calories 279; Fat 9 gm; Cholesterol 86 mg; Sodium 309 mg;
Food exchange value: 2 lean meat, 1 1/2 bread/starch, 2 vegetable

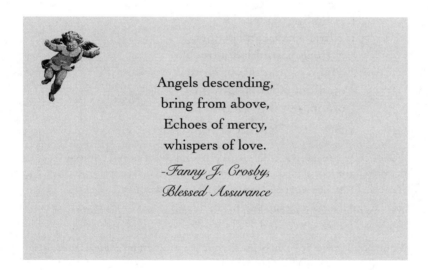

Angels descending,
bring from above,
Echoes of mercy,
whispers of love.

-Fanny J. Crosby,
Blessed Assurance

Flying Turkey Stir-Fry

4 servings — 2 cups each

1 lb. fresh boneless turkey breast
2 Tbsp. cornstarch, separated
5 Tbsp. white wine Worcestershire sauce, separated
1 clove garlic, minced
1 1/4 c. reduced-sodium chicken broth, defatted
1 c. boiling water
1/2 lb. fresh bean sprouts
2 c. finely shredded lettuce
2 Tbsp. canola oil, separated
2 medium carrots, shredded
1 onion, cut into chunks
2 tsp. slivered fresh ginger root

Cut turkey breast into thin strips. In a medium bowl, combine
1 tablespoon cornstarch and 2 tablespoons Worcestershire with garlic. Stir in turkey strips. Let stand 10 to 15 minutes.

Meanwhile, combine chicken broth, remaining 3 tablespoons of
Worcestershire sauce, and 1 tablespoon cornstarch; set aside.

Pour boiling water over bean sprouts in a bowl; let stand 1 minute.
Drain and rinse under cold water, then drain again thoroughly. Toss
bean sprouts with lettuce. Line a serving platter with the lettuce
mixture; set aside.

Heat 1 tablespoon oil over high heat in a wok or large skillet. Add turkey, and stir-fry 2 minutes; remove. Heat remaining 1 tablespoon oil in the same pan. Add carrots, onion, and ginger, and stir-fry 4 minutes. Add turkey and Worcestershire sauce mixture. Cook and stir until sauce boils and thickens. Turn out onto the lettuce-lined platter.

Nutrients per serving:
Calories 245; Fat 10 gm; Cholesterol 61 mg; Sodium 210 mg;
Food exchange value: 4 lean meat, 1 vegetable

"Matthew, Mark, Luke, and John
The bed be blest that I lie on
Four angels to my bed,
Four angels round my head,
One to watch and one to pray,
And two to beat my soul away."

-Thomas Ady, A Candle in the Dark

Cherub's Hot Chili Pie

6 servings — 1/6 of pie each

Vegetable oil cooking spray
2 c. boiling water
2 medium baking potatoes, cut into small cubes
1 lb. ground turkey or lean ground beef
1 tsp. chili powder
1 tsp. dried oregano
6-oz. can tomato paste
1 medium onion, finely chopped
1/2 c. egg substitute
15-oz. can hot chili beans, drained
4-oz. can diced green chilies, drained
1/2 c. shredded reduced-fat cheddar cheese
Garnish: shredded lettuce, diced tomato

Spray a 9-inch oven-safe glass pie plate with cooking spray. Preheat the oven to 375°.

Place potato cubes in boiling water, and boil for approximately 15 minutes, until potatoes are tender. Rinse under hot water, and drain.

In a large skillet, brown ground turkey or beef; drain. Add chili powder, oregano, tomato paste, and onion. Cook over medium heat for 3 to 4 minutes, until onion pieces are tender. Remove from heat, and stir in egg substitute. Place meat mixture along bottom and up the sides of the pie plate to form a shell.

In a medium bowl, gently stir together chili beans and green chilies. Place beans inside the meat shell forming an outer ring.

Toss together potato cubes and cheddar cheese in a medium bowl. Place in the center of the meat shell. Bake for 35 minutes, or until edges of meat shell are lightly browned and potato cubes are tender.

Garnish with shredded lettuce and diced tomato, if desired.

Nutrients per serving:

Calories 297; Fat 9 gm; Cholesterol 46 mg; Sodium 465 mg;
Food exchange value: 1 1/2 bread/starch, 3 lean meat, 1 vegetable

"The Son was made greater than the angels,
just as the name that God gave him is
greater than theirs."

-Hebrews 1:4

Seraphim
Seafood Kabobs

6 servings — 2 skewers each

2 dozen large sea scallops
1 dozen medium shrimp, peeled and deveined
1 dozen pearl onions, peeled, rinsed, and drained
1 large yellow bell pepper, cut into 2-inch pieces
2 Tbsp. olive oil
1/4 c. lime juice
3 cups hot cooked rice
Vegetable oil cooking spray

Combine all ingredients except rice in a large bowl, and toss gently. Alternately thread scallops, shrimp, onions, and bell pepper on each of 12 skewers. Reserve marinade.

Spray a broiler pan with cooking spray. Place kabobs on the pan, and brush with marinade. Place approximately 4 inches from broiler, and broil 6 to 8 minutes, turning twice, until scallops are opaque and shrimp is pink. Serve over rice.

Nutrients per serving:
Calories 232; Fat 5 gm; Cholesterol 42 mg; Sodium 119 mg;
Food exchange value: 1 1/2 lean meat, 2 bread/starch

Side Dishes

Singing Spinach Soufflé

8 servings — 1 cup each

2 Tbsp. reduced-fat soft margarine
1/4 c. flour
1/4 tsp. salt
1/4 tsp. white pepper
1/2 tsp. rosemary
1 c. skim milk
1/4 c. soft cheddar cheese food (such as Kraft
   Spreadery)
2 Tbsp. grated onion
1/4 tsp. salt
3 whole eggs, separated*
1/4 tsp. cream of tartar
10 oz. frozen spinach, thawed and squeezed dry
Vegetable oil cooking spray

Preheat oven to 400°. Melt margarine in a medium saucepan. Stir in flour, salt, pepper, and rosemary. Over medium heat, slowly pour in milk. Continue stirring until mixture thickens, then remove from heat. Stir in soft cheese and grated onion.

Separate eggs. Beat whites with cream of tartar until they're stiff; set aside. In a small bowl, beat yolks until very thick and lemon colored, then stir into the white sauce mixture. Fold spinach into the white sauce mixture. Stir 1/4 of the egg whites into the white sauce mixture, then very gently fold in the remaining whites. Carefully transfer to a soufflé or casserole dish that has been sprayed with cooking spray.

Set the dish in a baking pan of 1-inch deep water. Bake for 45 to 50 minutes, or until lightly browned. Serve immediately.

*Whole eggs are recommended for this recipe rather than liquid egg substitute.

Nutrients per serving:
Calories 98; Fat 4 gm; Cholesterol 83 mg; Sodium 423 mg;
Food exchange value: 2 vegetable, 1 lean meat

"Everyone entrusted with a mission
is an angel. . . . All forces that reside in
the body are angels."

-Moses Maimonides

"God will give orders to his angels about you;
they will hold you up with their hands, so that
not even your feet will be hurt on the stones."

-Matthew 4:6

Praise the Sweet
Potato Casserole

8 servings — 3/4 cup each

6 sweet potatoes
1 tsp. margarine
2 eggs or 1/2 c. liquid egg substitute
1/4 c. brown sugar
1/4 c. evaporated skim milk
1 tsp. cinnamon
1/2 tsp. nutmeg
1 tsp. vanilla
2 Tbsp. chopped pecans (optional)

Cut the potatoes in half, cover with water, and boil for 20 minutes in their skins. Then cool and peel. Mash cooked potatoes with remaining casserole ingredients, and transfer to an 11" x 8" casserole dish. Sprinkle with pecans, if desired. Microwave on high power for 10 minutes or bake in a preheated conventional oven at 400° for 20 to 25 minutes.

Nutrients per serving without pecans:
Calories 145; Fat 2 gm; Cholesterol 53 mg; Sodium 37 mg;
Food exchange value: 2 bread/starch

"The blessed damosel leaned out from
the gold bar of heaven."

-Dante Rossetti, The Blessed Damosel

All's Righteous Potatoes

12 servings — 1/2 cup each

6 large potatoes
13-oz. can reduced-fat cream of chicken soup
1 c. nonfat sour cream
4 green onions, chopped
2 oz. reduced-fat cheddar cheese, shredded

Cut the potatoes in half, cover with water, and boil for 20 minutes in their skins. Then drain, peel, and dice. In a large mixing bowl, combine soup and sour cream. Fold in the diced potatoes. Transfer to an 11" x 7" casserole dish. Sprinkle with green onions and shredded cheese. Microwave on high power for 15 minutes or bake in a preheated conventional oven at 400° for 20 to 25 minutes.

Nutrients per serving:

Calories 157; Fat 2 gm; Cholesterol 3 mg; Sodium 155 mg;
Food exchange value: 2 bread/starch

"Angels get to earth by sliding
down sunbeams."

-Common angel legend

Miracle Veggies
on the Grill

8 servings—3/4 cup each

6 c. assorted fresh vegetable chunks
(recommend a combination of peppers, small
onions, mushrooms, zucchini, cherry tomatoes,
new potatoes, or yellow squash)

Sauce for grilling:
1 Tbsp. brown sugar
2 Tbsp. teriyaki sauce
2 Tbsp. orange juice
1 Tbsp. ketchup

Prepare vegetables, and set aside. Combine ingredients for sauce in
a small mixing bowl. Place vegetables on skewers or directly on the
grate for grilling. Brush vegetables with sauce. Grill 5 to 7 minutes,
then turn and brush the other side. Grill 4 to 5 minutes more. Serve
with hamburgers.

Nutrients per serving:
*Calories 30; Fat 0; Cholesterol 0; Sodium 169 mg;
Food exchange value: 1 vegetable*

"See that you don't despise any of these
little ones. Their angels in heaven,
I tell you, are always in the presence of my
Father in heaven."

-Matthew 18:10

Church Potluck Zucchini Slaw

*Throw this potluck favorite together on
Sunday morning with common ingredients.*

8 servings — 1 cup each

6 slices bacon
3 medium zucchini, grated (may substitute potato)
2 large carrots, grated
1 medium onion, grated
1/2 tsp. salt
2 Tbsp. sugar
1/3 c. cider vinegar
1 tsp. caraway seeds

In a large skillet, cook bacon until crisp. Remove bacon to a paper towel, and discard drippings from the pan. Add grated zucchini, carrots, and onion to the pan. Stir in salt, and stir-fry over medium heat for 4 minutes. (If you are using potatoes, increase heating time to 10 minutes.) Sprinkle vegetables with sugar and vinegar, and heat over high heat until vinegar is evaporated. Crumble bacon and add to the mixture along with caraway seeds. Serve warm in a covered casserole dish or serve at room temperature as a slaw.

Nutrients per serving:
*Calories 59; Fat 2 gm; Cholesterol 4 mg; Sodium 346 mg;
Food exchange value: 1 vegetable, 1/2 fat*

"There is an unseen hand, a guiding angel,
that somehow, like a submerged propeller,
drives us on."

-Rabindranath Tagore

Billowy Swiss Green Beans

8 servings — 1 cup each

1 medium onion, chopped
1 green pepper, chopped
1 Tbsp. margarine
8-oz. can sliced mushrooms, drained
1 c. nonfat sour cream
3 16-oz. cans kitchen-cut green beans, drained
4 oz. reduced-fat Swiss cheese, shredded
1 Tbsp. sugar
1/2 tsp. pepper

Preheat oven to 350°. Sauté onion and green pepper in margarine in a large skillet. Add mushrooms, sour cream, beans, and cheese. Mix well. Add sugar and pepper. Spoon into a casserole dish, and bake for 30 minutes.

Nutrients per serving:
Calories 127; Fat 4 gm; Cholesterol 10 mg; Sodium 153 mg;
Food exchange value: 3 vegetable, 1 fat

"In the same way, I tell you, the angels of God
rejoice over one sinner who repents."

-Luke 15:10

Cabbage in a Cheese Robe

8 servings — 1 cup each

1 large head green cabbage, cleaned and cut into
    1/2-inch strips
13-oz. can reduced-fat cream of celery soup
4 oz. reduced-fat Cheddar cheese, shredded
1/2 c. nonfat sour cream
1 tsp. white pepper
1 c. dried bread crumbs
1 Tbsp. melted margarine

Preheat oven to 350°. Bring 3 quarts of water to a boil in a large
kettle with a steamer insert. Add strips of cabbage to the steamer
insert, and heat over boiling water for 8 minutes. Transfer steamed
cabbage to a large casserole dish. If you prefer microwave steaming,
sprinkle cabbage with 1/4 cup of water in a covered dish, and cook
on high power for 5 minutes.

While the cabbage is steaming, combine soup, shredded cheese, sour
cream, and pepper in a small mixing bowl. Fold into cooked cabbage. Combine bread crumbs and melted margarine, and sprinkle
over the top. Bake for 25 minutes or until the mixture is bubbly.

Nutrients per serving:
Calories 154; Fat 6 gm; Cholesterol 12 mg; Sodium 370 mg;
Food exchange value: 1 vegetable, 1 skim milk, 1 fat

Inspiring
Celery Victoria

8 servings — 1 round each

2 large bunches of celery
10-oz. can no-added-salt beef broth
2 Tbsp. vegetable oil
3 Tbsp. cider vinegar
1 Tbsp. water
1 Tbsp. fresh minced parsley
1/4 tsp. minced garlic
1/2 tsp. basil
1/2 tsp. oregano
1/4 tsp. curry powder
1/2 tsp. salt
1/4 tsp. pepper
2 Tbsp. chopped pimiento

Clean celery thoroughly without pulling stalks apart. Trim off the root end, still leaving stalks together. Cut 2-inch rounds of stalks, starting at the trimmed end. Use a string to tie the rounds of stalks together. Reserve the tops of the celery bunch for another use.

Stack the bound celery rounds in a large pot. Add broth, and steam over medium heat for 10 minutes. If you prefer the microwave method, place celery rounds in a microwave casserole dish, sprinkle with broth, cover, and cook on high power for 7 minutes.

Remove steamed celery bunches with a slotted spoon to a dish that can be covered. Combine all remaining ingredients in a shaker container. Pour dressing over the celery rounds, and marinate in the refrigerator for at least 3 hours. Serve as a cold side dish with meats.

Nutrients per serving:
Calories 73; Fat 3 gm; Cholesterol 0; Sodium 135 mg;
Food exchange value: 2 vegetable, 1/2 fat

"It is only with the heart that one can see rightly; what is essential is invisible to the eye."

-Antoine de Saint-Exupery,
The Little Prince

"There is a land of pure delight
Where saints immortal reign
Infinite day excludes the night
And pleasures banish pain."

Isaac Watts, There Is a Land

Tangy Cauliflower Crowns

8 servings — 3/4 cup each

1 large head cauliflower, cleaned and trimmed
2 Tbsp. water
1/4 c. reduced-fat mayonnaise
1 tsp. grated onion
1 tsp. prepared mustard
2 oz. reduced-fat Cheddar cheese, shredded

Place the whole cauliflower in a casserole dish. Add water, and cover with plastic wrap. Microwave on high power for 8 minutes. Drain. In a small mixing bowl, combine mayonnaise, onion, and mustard. Spoon over the steamed and drained cauliflower, then sprinkle with cheese. Microwave uncovered for 2 more minutes. Let stand for 2 minutes before cutting and serving.

Nutrients per serving:

Calories 75; Fat 4 gm; Cholesterol 5 mg; Sodium 135 mg;
Food exchange value: 1 fat, 1 vegetable

Fiery Eggplant Creole

6 servings—1 cup each

Vegetable oil cooking spray
1 medium eggplant
1 Tbsp. lemon juice
2 c. water
2 tsp. salt
3 Tbsp. margarine
3 Tbsp. flour
1/2 tsp. cayenne pepper*
1/2 tsp. ground cumin*
2 c. chopped fresh tomatoes
1 small green pepper, seeded and chopped
1 small white onion, chopped
1 Tbsp. brown sugar
2 Tbsp. unseasoned bread crumbs
3 Tbsp. grated Parmesan cheese

Spray a 9" x 13" baking dish with cooking spray. Preheat oven to 350°.

Peel and dice eggplant, and place in a small bowl. Drizzle with lemon juice, and toss gently to coat. Bring water and 1 teaspoon salt to boiling in a medium saucepan. Add eggplant, and boil 10 minutes. Drain. Place eggplant in prepared dish.

In the same saucepan, melt margarine. Add flour, cayenne, cumin, tomatoes, green pepper, onion, 1 teaspoon salt, and brown sugar. Cook for 5 minutes over medium heat. Pour sauce over eggplant. Sprinkle eggplant with bread crumbs and Parmesan cheese. Bake for 30 minutes.

*The eggplant and cooking methods bring out the heat of the cayenne and cumin in this recipe. If you prefer a slightly milder flavor, reduce cayenne and cumin to 1/4 teaspoon each.

Nutrients per serving:

Calories 99; Fat 3 gm; Cholesterol 7 mg; Sodium 378 mg; Food exchange value: 3 vegetable, 1/2 fat

Bugler's Kugel
12 servings—3/4 cup each

Vegetable oil cooking spray
1/2 tsp. allspice
1/2 c. sugar
8 oz. nonfat cottage cheese
3/4 tsp. vanilla
1 1/2 c. skim milk
3/4 c. egg substitute
1 c. nonfat sour cream
2 Tbsp. margarine, melted
1/2 lb. broad noodles, cooked and drained

Topping:
1/2 c. lightly crushed corn flakes
2 tsp. cinnamon
1 tsp. sugar

Spray a 9" x 13" pan with cooking spray.

In a large bowl, combine allspice, sugar, cottage cheese, vanilla, and milk. Blend well. Stir in egg substitute. Add sour cream, margarine and noodles. Stir until noodles are well coated. Pour mixture into the prepared pan, and refrigerate overnight.

When ready to bake, preheat oven to 350°. Mix together topping ingredients in a small bowl. Sprinkle over the noodle mixture. Bake for 1 1/2 hours or until golden brown. Serve hot or cold, as a side dish or dessert.

Nutrients per serving:
Calories 191; Fat 4 gm; Cholesterol 2 mg; Sodium 185 mg;
Food exchange value: 2 bread/starch, 1/2 fat

"Unless you can love, as the angels may
With the breadth of heaven betwixt you;
Unless you can dream that his faith is fast,
Through behoving and unbehoving;
Unless you can die when the dream is past—
Oh, never call it loving!"

-Robert Browning, A Woman's Shortcomings

"They will be angels and cannot die."

-*Luke 20:36*

Acorn Squash Halos

6 servings — 2 slices each

3 acorn squash
2 Tbsp. margarine
1/4 c. firmly packed brown sugar
2 Tbsp. maple syrup
1/2 tsp. salt

Heat oven to 350°. Cut off both ends of each squash. Remove seeds and loose pulp. Slice squash into 4 1-inch thick rings. Arrange squash rings in a 13" x 9" (3-quart) baking dish; cover with foil. Bake for 35 to 40 minutes, until squash is nearly tender.

Melt margarine in a small saucepan. Stir in brown sugar, maple syrup, and salt. Cook over medium heat, stirring constantly, until sugar is just dissolved.

Spoon sauce over squash. Return baking dish, uncovered, to oven. Bake an additional 10 to 15 minutes, or until squash is very tender, basting occasionally. Let stand 5 minutes before serving.

Nutrients per serving:
*Calories 130; Fat 4 gm; Cholesterol 0; Sodium 241 mg;
Food exchange value: 1 bread/starch, 1/2 fruit, 1/2 fat*

Glory Beans
10 servings — 1/2 cup each

2 c. water
3 c. fresh green beans, strings and ends removed
3/4 c. water
1 tsp. dried oregano
1 tsp. dried basil
1/4 tsp. salt
1 tsp. dry mustard
1/4 c. white wine vinegar
1 Tbsp. olive oil
16 oz. can chick-peas (garbanzo beans), rinsed,
    and drained
6 slices red onion, separated into rings

Pour 2 cups water into a medium saucepan. Place green beans in a steamer basket, and place over water in saucepan. Cover and bring water to a boil, steaming for 10 minutes or until beans are crisp-tender.

Combine oregano, basil, salt, dry mustard, vinegar, and olive oil in a shaker container. Cover and shake to blend well. Set aside.

In 1 1/2 quart casserole, combine green beans and garbanzo beans. Shake dressing again, and pour over beans. Stir to coat. Place onion rings on beans. Cover and refrigerate at least 20 minutes before serving.

Nutrients per serving:
Calories 76; Fat 2 gm; Cholesterol 0; Sodium 197 mg;
Food exchange value: 1 vegetable, 1/2 bread/starch

"The angels sing the praise of their Lord and
ask forgiveness for those on earth. . . ."

-The Koran XLII:5

"God sends meat and the devil sends cooks."

-John Taylor, Works

Exalted Potatoes

12 servings — 1/2 cup each

Vegetable oil cooking spray
8 oz. nonfat cream cheese, softened
4 c. prepared mashed potatoes
1/3 c. grated onion
1/4 c. drained pimiento, chopped
1 egg, beaten, or 1/4 c. liquid egg substitute
1 tsp. celery salt
1 Tbsp. basil
2 tsp. dill weed

Spray 1 1/2-quart casserole with cooking spray. Preheat oven to 350°.

Combine cream cheese and mashed potatoes. Beat with an electric mixer until smooth. Add onion, pimiento, egg, celery salt, basil, and dill weed. Mix well.

Transfer to the prepared casserole, and bake for 45 minutes.

Nutrients per serving:

Calories 75; Fat 1 gm; Cholesterol 19 mg with egg, 0 with egg substitute; Sodium 395 mg; Food exchange value: 1 bread/starch

Gabriel's Lily Bake
(Asparagus/Kohlrabi Medley)
4 servings — 1 cup each

1 lb. fresh asparagus spears
2 c. water
2 medium kohlrabies
1 Tbsp. finely chopped fresh ginger root
1 Tbsp. vegetable oil
1 Tbsp. reduced-sodium soy sauce
1 Tbsp. white wine vinegar
1 Tbsp. brown sugar
Garnish: paprika

Wash asparagus spears, and break off woody bases where spears snap easily. Discard bases. Pour 2 cups of water in a large saucepan. Place asparagus spears in a steamer basket, and place in the saucepan. Bring water to a boil, and cook asparagus, covered, for 5 minutes, until spears are just tender. Uncover, remove from heat, and set aside.

Pare the large bulb of the kohlrabies, and discard the tops. Using a paring knife, carve 6 triangular grooves, approximately 1/4-inch apart, lengthwise down the sides of each kohlrabi bulb. Slice bulbs, and place slices in a microwave-safe 2-quart casserole. Add ginger root and oil. Cover and microwave on full power for 7 to 8 minutes, stirring once.

While kohlrabies are cooking, combine soy sauce, vinegar, and brown sugar in a small bowl. Set aside.

Add asparagus spears to kohlrabi. Stir soy sauce mixture, and pour over asparagus. Lightly toss to coat. Cover and return to microwave on high an additional 4 minutes, stirring twice.

Arrange on serving plates with asparagus spears for "stems" and kohlrabi slices for "flowers." Sprinkle kohlrabi with paprika if desired.

Nutrients per serving:

Calories 73; Fat 3 gm; Cholesterol 0; Sodium 132 mg;
Food exchange value: 2 vegetable, 1/2 fat

The Choir's Curried Rice

8 servings — 1/2 cup each

Vegetable oil cooking spray
2 c. water
3 medium carrots, cleaned and diced
1 Tbsp. olive oil
2 Tbsp. chopped yellow bell pepper
2 large cloves garlic, minced
1 small white onion, finely chopped
1 c. long grain white rice
14-oz. can reduced-sodium chicken broth
1 Tbsp. lemon juice
2 tsp. curry powder
1/2 tsp. ground ginger
1/2 tsp. ground thyme
1 small apple, peeled, cored, and diced (1/3 c.)
1/4 c. unsweetened apple juice

Spray a 2 1/2-quart oven-safe casserole with cooking spray. Bring water and carrots to boil in a large saucepan. Cook for 10 minutes. Drain and set aside. Preheat oven to 375°.

Warm oil over medium heat in a large skillet. Sauté yellow pepper, garlic, and onion until softened but not brown. Add rice, and sauté for 2 additional minutes, stirring often. Add broth, lemon juice, curry powder, ginger, and thyme. Heat to simmering. Transfer to the prepared casserole. Cover and bake for 15 minutes.

Remove casserole from oven, and stir in carrots, chopped apple, and apple juice. Return covered casserole to oven for an additional 10 minutes. Remove from oven and let stand, covered, for 5 to 7 minutes before serving.

Nutrients per serving:

Calories 122; Fat 2 gm; Cholesterol 0; Sodium 3 mg;
Food exchange value: 1 1/2 bread/starch

"(Mary) saw two angels there
dressed in white, sitting where the body
of Jesus had been, one at the head
and the other at the feet."

-John 20:12

Celestial Wax Beans

6 servings—2/3 cup each

1 1/2 lb. wax beans, cleaned and snipped
1 Tbsp. olive oil
2 cloves garlic, crushed
1 Tbsp. chopped yellow onion
1/4 c. diced red bell pepper
1/4 c. diced yellow bell pepper
1 c. water
1 tsp. salt
1 Tbsp. crushed basil
1/4 c. Parmesan cheese

Leave beans whole, or cut into 1-inch pieces. In a large skillet, heat oil and garlic. Add onions, and cook slowly for 3 minutes. Add bell peppers, beans, water, salt, and basil. Cover and simmer until beans are tender (15 to 20 minutes). Drain beans.

Stir in half of the Parmesan cheese. Turn into a serving dish, and top with remaining Parmesan.

Nutrients per serving:
Calories 68; Fat 4 gm; Cholesterol 5 mg; Sodium 429 mg;
Food exchange value: 1 fat, 1 vegetable

Desserts

"We may live without poetry, music and art;
We may live without conscience
and live without heart;
We may live without friends;
we may live without books;
But civilized man cannot live without cooks."

-Owen Meredith, Lucile

Angel Food Temptation
16 servings — 1 slice each

18-oz. angel food cake mix
1 c. nonfat sour cream
1/4 c. sugar
1 tsp. almond extract
1 c. low-fat strawberry yogurt
2 c. fresh strawberries, cleaned, stemmed,
    and cut into fourths
2 drops red food coloring
Garnish: whole strawberries or finely grated
    chocolate

Prepare cake mix as directed in a tube pan. When cake is cooled, trim brown crust, and remove from pan. Cut the cake into three layers, using a serrated knife.

Combine all remaining ingredients in a medium mixing bowl; blend well. Spread 1/3 of the strawberry mixture between each layer and on top of the cake. Garnish the top with whole fresh berries or finely grated chocolate. Chill until ready to serve.

This dessert may be prepared up to 6 hours before serving and will keep its form in the refrigerator for 24 hours.

Nutrients per serving:
Calories 143; Fat 0; Cholesterol 0; Sodium 218 mg;
Food exchange value: 1 bread/starch, 1 fruit

"Remember the angels who do not stay within
the limits of their proper authority."

-Jude 6

Pineapple Pinnacle Cake
24 servings — 1 square each

94% fat-free yellow cake mix (such as Duncan
   Hines DeLights)
1/4 c. sugar
20-oz. can crushed pineapple in juice
2 3-oz. pkg. sugar-free instant vanilla pudding
2 c. low-fat buttermilk
Garnish: 1/4 c. slivered almonds

Prepare cake in a 9" x 13" pan as directed on package.

In a small saucepan, combine sugar with pineapple and juice. Bring
to a boil, then reduce heat to low. Simmer for 10 minutes or until
pineapple has thickened. Transfer thickened pineapple to a bowl to
cool. In the same saucepan, combine vanilla pudding and buttermilk. Bring mixture to a boil, and boil for a full 2 minutes.

When cake has cooled, punch holes in the cake with a straw. Pour
pineapple mixture over the top. Spread the pudding over the
pineapple, and garnish with almonds.

Nutrients per serving:
*Calories 85; Fat 2 gm; Cholesterol 1 mg; Sodium 149 mg;
Food exchange value: 1 bread/starch*

"He will do this when the Lord Jesus appears
from heaven with his mighty angels."

-II Thessalonians 1:7

Heavenly Orange Fluff

12 servings — 1/12 pan each

2 3-oz. pkg. sugar-free orange gelatin
1 c. boiling water
6 oz. frozen orange juice concentrate
11-oz. can mandarin oranges, drained
20-oz. can crushed pineapple
1 pkg. sugar-free instant vanilla pudding
1 c. skim milk
2 Tbsp. sugar-free lemonade drink mix or 2 tsp.
   finely grated lemon peel
Optional garnish: twisted fresh orange slices

In a medium mixing bowl, dissolve gelatin in boiling water. Add orange juice concentrate, drained oranges, and undrained pineapple and juice. Pour into a 13" x 9" pan, and refrigerate.

In a small saucepan, combine pudding mix and milk. Cook over medium heat, stirring constantly. Boil mixture for 1 minute or until thick. Stir in lemonade drink mix or lemon peel.

Before serving, frost gelatin with lemon pudding. Garnish salad plates with twisted fresh orange slices.

Nutrients per serving:
Calories 70; Fat 0; Cholesterol 0; Sodium 105 mg;
Food exchange value: 1 bread/starch

Guardian Angel
"'Tis said we are blessed
With a guardian angel in disguise
We do not always know them,
For they appear in any form or size.
They do arrive when needed,
In a strange, mysterious way,
Not by chance as some may think,
But on a special day.
So if you are sad with no direction
As to what course to pursue,
Just wait for your protection
From an angel meant just for you."

-Mary M. Wadham

Angel Cubes
24 servings — 1/24 of recipe each

1 angel food cake mix
8 oz. fat-free cream cheese
1 tsp. vanilla
1/4 c. sugar
2 c. flake cereal with almonds (such as Almond
   Delight), crushed

Prepare cake per package directions in two 9-inch loaf pans. Cool and remove from pan, then cut cake into 2-inch cubes. Line a baking sheet with wax paper; set aside.

Soften cream cheese to room temperature by resting the container in hot tap water for a few minutes. Mix the cream cheese with the vanilla and sugar in a small bowl. Frost the sides of the cake cubes with the cream cheese mixture, then roll in crushed cereal. Place the frosted cake cubes on the wax paper-lined baking sheet to set. Refrigerate until serving time.

Nutrients per serving:
Calories 88; Fat 0; Cholesterol 0; Sodium 159 mg;
Food exchange value: 1 bread/starch

"Then war broke out in heaven.
Michael and his angels fought against the
dragon who fought back with his angels."

-Revelation 12:7

Devil's Food Redemption Cake

24 servings — 1/24 of cake each

Vegetable oil cooking spray
2 c. miniature marshmallows
1/4 c. chopped pecans
1/3 c. brown sugar
1/2 c. cocoa
1 c. hot water
18-oz. pkg. reduced-fat devil's food cake mix
3 eggs or 3/4 c. liquid egg substitute
Water

Preheat oven to 350°. Spray the bottom of a 13" x 9" cake pan with cooking spray. Sprinkle marshmallows and pecans in the pan. In a small bowl, combine sugar, cocoa, and hot water. Stir to mix, then pour over marshmallows. Prepare cake with eggs and water according to package directions. Pour over marshmallow layer. Bake for 40 minutes or until cake tests done.

Nutrients per serving:
Calories 150; Fat 2 gm; Cholesterol 27 mg with egg, 0 with egg substitute; Sodium 167 mg; Food exchange value: 2 bread/starch

Angel Food Cake From Scratch

12 servings — 1/12 of cake each

1 1/8 c. cake flour, sifted
3/4 c. sugar
1 1/2 c. egg whites, at room temperature
1/2 tsp. salt
1 1/2 tsp. cream of tartar
1 c. sugar
1 tsp. vanilla
1/4 tsp. almond extract

Preheat oven to 350°. Sift together cake flour and 3/4 c. sugar five times. Beat room temperature egg whites to slightly foamy stage. Add salt and cream of tartar. Continue beating at high speed until stiff but not dry. Reduce speed, and sprinkle sugar, vanilla, and almond extract over the batter. As soon as the sugar isn't heard (about 1 minute), reduce speed. Then slowly mix in the flour and sugar mixture, about 1 1/2 minutes.

Carefully transfer batter to a 10-inch tube pan. Use a knife to cut through batter to break air pockets. Bake for 35 minutes or until the top is golden. Hang the cake upside down for 1 hour or until it is cool to the touch. Then transfer to a serving platter.

Nutrients per serving:
Calories 155; Fat 0; Cholesterol 0; Sodium 89 mg;
Food exchange value: 2 bread/starch

"Rebellious angels are worse
than unbelieving men."

-Voltaire

"We not only live among men,
but there are airy hosts, blessed spectators,
sympathetic lookers-on, that see and know and
appreciate our thoughts and feelings and acts."

-Henry Ward Beecher,
Royal Truths

Holy Scripture Cake

24 servings — 1/24 of cake each

Vegetable oil cooking spray
2 c. Jeremiah 6:20 (sugar)
1/2 c. Judges 5:25 (soft margarine)
6 Jeremiah 17:11 (eggs)
4 1/2 c. I Kings 4:22 (flour)
2 tsp. Amos 4:5 (baking powder)
2 tsp. Leviticus 2:13 (salt)
1/2 c. Judges 4:19 (milk)
1/2 c. Numbers 17:8 (almonds)
2 c. Nahum 3:12 (chopped dried fruit)
2 tsp. II Chronicles 9:9 (cinnamon)

Preheat oven to 350°. Spray a 9" x 13" cake pan with cooking spray.

Cream sugar and margarine in a large mixing bowl until smooth.
Beat in eggs one at a time. Combine flour, baking powder, and salt
in a small mixing bowl. Add alternately with milk to the egg and
sugar mixture. Fold in almonds, dried fruit, and cinnamon. Bake for
30 minutes.

Nutrients per serving:

Calories 189; Fat 5 gm; Cholesterol 53 mg; Sodium 245 mg;
Food exchange value: 1 bread/starch, 1 fruit, 1 fat

"A ministering angel shall my sister be."

-*William Shakespeare, Hamlet*

Bananas Among the Clouds

8 servings—1 meringue square each

4 egg whites
1 c. sugar
1 tsp. vanilla extract
1/4 tsp. vinegar
1 1/2 c. mashed bananas
1/4 tsp. salt
1 1/2 Tbsp. lemon juice
2 c. nonfat vanilla frozen yogurt, softened
Garnish: fresh mint leaves

Preheat oven to 275°. Beat egg whites in a medium mixing bowl until nearly stiff. Gradually add sugar, beating constantly. Add vanilla and vinegar. Beat until stiff and well blended. Divide the meringue in half. Spread each half over a 3- by 8-inch area of a baking sheet. Bake for 40 minutes or until delicately browned. Remove from the oven, and cool.

Combine bananas, salt, and lemon juice. Fold softened frozen yogurt into the banana mixture. Place one meringue in a freezer-safe tray, and cover with filling. Top with the second meringue. Freeze for 3 hours. Cut into 8 portions, and decorate the top with fresh mint.

Nutrients per serving:
Calories 186; Fat 0; Cholesterol 0; Sodium 89 mg;
Food exchange value: 3 fruit

"Millions of spiritual
creatures walk the earth
unseen, both when we wake
and when we sleep."

-John Milton, Paradise Lost

Yellow Angel Food Cake From Scratch

This angel food cake recipe uses the whole egg instead of just the white.
12 servings — 1 wedge each

6 eggs, separated
1/2 c. cold water
1 1/2 c. sugar
1 1/2 c. cake flour
1 1/2 tsp. baking powder
1/4 tsp. salt
1 tsp. vanilla
3/4 tsp. cream of tartar

Preheat oven to 300°. In a large mixing bowl, beat egg yolks well for 4 minutes. Beat cold water into the eggs. Add sugar, and beat again. Sift flour, baking powder, and salt together two times. Add to the egg mixture. Fold in vanilla. In a medium mixing bowl, beat egg whites with cream of tartar until stiff. When egg whiles are stiff, fold them into the egg yolk batter. Transfer batter carefully to a 10-inch tube pan.

Bake for 15 minutes in a 300° oven, then increase heat to 350°, and continue baking for 1 more hour.

Nutrients per serving:
Calories 217; Fat 3 gm; Cholesterol 106 mg; Sodium 122 mg;
Food exchange value: 2 bread/starch, 1 fruit

August 22 is called "Be an Angel Day."
On that day, people do special and anonymous
favors for one another.

Pink Cloud

8 servings — 1/2 cup each

20-oz. can crushed pineapple in juice
2 Tbsp. sugar
3-oz. package sugar-free raspberry gelatin (may use
    regular gelatin)
16 oz. nonfat ricotta cheese
1 c. cold vanilla yogurt

Combine pineapple and sugar in a medium saucepan, and heat to boiling. Stir in gelatin. Remove from heat, and stir until gelatin is dissolved. Cool to room temperature, then fold in ricotta cheese and yogurt. Place in a dessert bowl, or portion in individual dessert dishes, and chill for at least 2 hours. Serve with a reduced-fat vanilla sandwich cookie.

Nutrients per serving (with sugar-free gelatin):
Calories 119; Fat 0; Cholesterol 7 mg; Sodium 47 mg;
Food exchange value: 2 fruit

"Angels are spirits, but it is not
because they are spirits that they
are angels. They become angels when
they are sent. For the name "angel" refers to
their office, not their nature. You ask the name
of this nature, it is spirit; you ask its office, it is
that of an angel, which is a messenger."

St. Augustine

Miraculous Pie

8 servings — 1/8 of pie each

Vegetable oil cooking spray
1 c. egg substitute
1/2 c. all-purpose flour
2 c. skim milk
2/3 c. flaked coconut
1/4 tsp. salt
1/2 tsp. baking powder
1 Tbsp. almond extract
1/2 tsp. ground ginger

Preheat oven to 375°. Spray a 10-inch pie plate with cooking spray.

Place all ingredients in a blender or food processor. Blend thoroughly. Pour batter into the prepared pie plate. Bake for 1 hour. A crust will "miraculously" form on the bottom, the milk mixture will form a pie filling, and the coconut will form a topping.

Nutrients per serving:
Calories 107; Fat 3 gm; Cholesterol 1 mg; Sodium 192 mg;
Food exchange value: 1 bread/starch, 1/2 fat

O'Heavenly Oatmeal Cake

18 servings — 1 slice each

Vegetable oil cooking spray
1 1/4 c. water
1 c. quick-cooking oats
1/2 c. apple juice
1/8 c. canola oil
1/2 c. granulated sugar
1/2 c. brown sugar
1/2 c. egg substitute
1 1/2 c. flour
1 tsp. baking soda
1 tsp. salt
2 1/2 tsp. cinnamon
1 tsp. nutmeg
1/2 Tbsp. vanilla extract

Preheat oven to 350°. Spray the bottom and only halfway up the sides of an angel food cake pan with cooking spray.

Bring water to a boil in a large saucepan. Stir in oats; let cool. In a large bowl, combine apple juice, oil, both sugars, and egg substitute. Stir in oats. In a small bowl, sift together flour, baking soda, salt, cinnamon, and nutmeg. Add to oat mixture. Stir in vanilla, and continue stirring until all ingredients are mixed well.

Pour into the prepared pan, and bake for 45 minutes, or until a toothpick inserted near the center comes out clean.

Nutrients per serving:

Calories 116; Fat 2 gm; Cholesterol 0; Sodium 184 mg;
Food exchange value: 1 bread/starch, 1/2 fruit

Pumpkin Angels

48 servings — 1 angel each

Vegetable oil cooking spray
1 c. all-purpose flour
1 c. whole wheat flour
1 1/2 c. sugar
2 tsp. baking powder
2 Tbsp. pumpkin pie spice
1 tsp. baking soda
1/4 tsp. salt
1 c. egg substitute
16-oz. can pumpkin
1/2 c. vegetable oil
2/3 c. nonfat plain yogurt
Garnish: powdered sugar

Preheat oven to 350°. Spray a 15" x 10" jelly roll pan with cooking spray.

In a large bowl, combine flours, sugar, baking powder, pumpkin pie spice, baking soda, and salt. Mix well. Stir in egg substitute, pumpkin, oil, and yogurt. Spread batter into the prepared pan.

Bake for 25 to 30 minutes, or until a toothpick inserted near the center comes out clean. Cool completely in the pan.

With a 1 1/2-inch angel cookie cutter, cut out little angel cakes, and place on a serving plate. Sprinkle with powdered sugar if desired.

Nutrients per serving:

Calories 70; Fat 1 gm; Cholesterol 0; Sodium 89 mg;
Food exchange value: 1 bread/starch

City of Angels Fruitcake

18 servings—1 slice each

Vegetable oil cooking spray
6 oz. dried fruit bits (1 1/2 cups)
2 c. water
1/2 c. nonfat sour cream
1 c. sugar
1/2 c. egg substitute
1 tsp. baking soda
1 1/2 tsp. baking powder
1 Tbsp. cinnamon
2 1/2 c. flour
1 c. applesauce
Garnish: 1 Tbsp. powdered sugar

Preheat oven to 350°. Spray the bottom and sides of a 9" x 5" loaf pan with cooking spray. Combine fruit bits and water in a medium saucepan. Bring to a boil, then remove from heat, and set aside for 10 minutes.

Mix the sour cream and sugar in a large bowl until smooth. Add egg substitute, and blend well. Stir in baking soda, baking powder, and cinnamon. Add flour alternately with applesauce, mixing well after each addition.

Drain water from fruit bits. Fold fruit bits into batter.

Pour batter into the prepared pan. Bake for 50 minutes, or until a toothpick inserted near the center comes out clean. Allow loaf to cool in pan for 10 minutes before turning out onto a serving plate. Sprinkle powdered sugar over top if desired.

Nutrients per serving:

Calories 153; Fat 1 gm; Cholesterol 0; Sodium 126 mg; Food exchange value: 1 bread/starch, 1 fruit

"Hold the fleet angel fast until he bless thee."

-Nathaniel Cotton, Tomorrow

Almond Cookie Wings

48 servings—1 "wing" each

2 Tbsp. margarine
8 oz. nonfat cream cheese
1/2 c. granulated sugar
1/2 c. firmly packed brown sugar
1/3 c. egg substitute
2 tsp. vanilla extract
2 c. all-purpose flour
1/2 tsp. baking powder
1/4 tsp. salt
Vegetable oil cooking spray
12-oz. can almond filling (not almond paste)
Powdered sugar (optional)

In a large mixing bowl, beat together margarine, cream cheese, and sugars until light and fluffy. Add egg and vanilla; beat until well blended. Stir in flour, baking powder, and salt. Divide dough in quarters. Wrap separately, and refrigerate 2 hours or overnight.

Preheat oven to 350°. Spray 2 cookie sheets with cooking spray. Roll each quarter of dough on a well-floured surface into a 12- by 6-inch rectangle. Spread one quarter of the almond filling down the center of each rectangle. Fold dough lengthwise in thirds over the filling. Using a metal spatula, transfer rolls, seam side down, to cookie sheets.

Bake for 15 to 20 minutes, or until lightly browned. Cool on wire racks. Cut each roll into 12 triangles. If desired, sprinkle lightly with powdered sugar before serving.

Nutrients per serving:
Calories 50; Fat 1 gm; Cholesterol 0; Sodium 18 mg;
Food exchange value: 1/2 bread/starch

"So many wings come here
dipping honey
and speak here
in your home, Oh God.

-Aztec poem

Celestial Fruit Pizza

12 servings — 1/12 of pizza each

Vegetable oil cooking spray
1 lb. loaf frozen bread dough, thawed
8-oz. package nonfat cream cheese, softened
1 egg
1 tsp. pure (not imitation) vanilla extract
11-oz. can mandarin oranges
2 kiwifruit
1/2 c. red seedless grapes, halved
2 Tbsp. honey (optional)

Preheat oven to 375°. Spray a 14-inch pizza pan with cooking spray. Roll bread dough to a 14-inch circle, and place on the prepared pan. Lightly prick crust with a fork.

Bake crust for 15 minutes. Remove from oven, and set pan on a wire rack. Prick any bubbles that may have formed in the crust with a fork.

Reduce oven temperature to 350°.

Combine cream cheese, egg, and vanilla extract in a medium bowl. Blend well. Spread cream cheese mixture evenly over bread dough. Bake at 350° for 20 minutes, until cream cheese is set and crust is just turning golden brown. Remove from oven to wire rack, and allow to cool for 5 minutes.

Drain juice from mandarin oranges. Peel kiwi, and slice into 1/4-inch thick rounds. Place mandarin orange "moons," kiwi "planets," and grape "asteroids" randomly on the cream cheese. Press gently into the cream cheese. Drizzle with honey, if desired.

Nutrients per serving (with honey):

Calories 110; Fat 1 gm; Cholesterol 17 mg; Sodium 136 mg; Food exchange value: 1/2 fruit, 1 bread/starch

"If I have freedom in my love,
And in my soul am free,
Angels alone that soar above
Enjoy such liberty."

-Richard Lovelace
To Althea From Prison

Sugar Angels

30 servings — 1 cookie each

1 c. powdered sugar
1/2 c. margarine
1/4 c. applesauce
1 tsp. vanilla extract
1 tsp. almond extract
2 1/2 c. all-purpose flour
1 tsp. baking soda
1 tsp. cream of tartar
Vegetable oil cooking spray

Angel icing (optional):
1/4 c. powdered sugar
3 drops yellow food coloring
2 tsp. water

In a large bowl, mix the powdered sugar, margarine, applesauce, vanilla, and almond extract thoroughly. Stir in the flour, baking soda, and cream of tartar. Cover and refrigerate 2 hours or until firm.

Spray 2 cookie sheets with cooking spray. Preheat oven to 375°. Roll half the dough at a time to a 1/4-inch thickness on a lightly floured surface. Cut out cookies with an angel-shaped cookie cutter, and place on cookie sheets.

Bake for 8 minutes, or until bottoms are lightly browned. Remove from the cookie sheet. Cool completely on a wire rack.

In small bowl, prepare icing, if desired, and brush over cookies with a pastry brush. Allow to dry (3 to 5 minutes) before serving.

Nutrients per serving (with icing):
Calories 85; Fat 3 gm; Cholesterol 0; Sodium 40 mg;
Food exchange value: 1 bread/starch

"Our acts our angels are, or good or ill,
Our fatal shadows that walk by still."

-John Fletcher,
The Honest Man's Fortune

"A cherub is a member of the second order of
angels often represented as a winged child."

-Gail Harvey, On the Wings of Angels

Lofty Lemon Cookies
24 servings — 1 cookie each

1/4 c. margarine
1/2 c. applesauce
1/2 c. powdered sugar
1 tsp. lemon extract
2 c. all-purpose flour
1/4 tsp. salt
1 Tbsp. grated lemon peel
Vegetable oil cooking spray
Granulated sugar

In a large bowl, combine the margarine, applesauce, powdered sugar, and lemon extract. Stir in flour, salt, and lemon peel. (If the dough is soft, cover and refrigerate 1 to 2 hours until firm enough to shape.)

Preheat oven to 400°. Spray 2 baking sheets with cooking spray.

Shape dough into 1-inch balls. Place about 1 inch apart on cookie sheets. Press balls slightly with the flat bottom of a glass dipped in granulated sugar. Bake 8 to 10 minutes or until bottoms are lightly browned. Remove from the cookie sheet immediately; cool completely on a wire rack.

Nutrients per serving:
Calories 68; Fat 2 gm; Cholesterol 0; Sodium 40 mg;
Food exchange value: 1 bread/starch

"An angel can illumine the thought and
mind of man by strengthening the power of
vision, and by bringing within its reach some
truth which the angel himself contemplates."

-Thomas Aquinas

Angel Kisses
48 servings — 1 kiss each

Vegetable oil cooking spray
4 egg whites
1/2 tsp. cream of tartar
1/4 tsp. salt
1 c. sugar
1 tsp. almond extract
1/2 tsp. rum flavoring

Preheat oven to 350°. Spray 2 cookie sheets with cooking spray.

In a medium bowl, beat egg whites with cream of tartar until stiff. Add salt and sugar, and beat again. Stir in flavorings. Drop batter by rounded teaspoonfuls onto prepared baking sheets.

Bake for 12 to 15 minutes, or until "kisses" are dry to the touch.

Nutrients per serving:
Calories 16; Fat 0; Cholesterol 0; Sodium 11 mg;
Food exchange value: 1 serving = free food; 2 kisses = 1/2 fruit

"But all God's angels come to us disguised:
sorrow and sickness, poverty and death,
One after another lift their frowning masks,
And we behold the seraph's face beneath,
All radiant with the glory and the calm
Of having looked upon the front of God."

-James Russell Lowell

Chocolate Angel Kisses

50 servings — 1 kiss each

Follow recipe for regular Angel Kisses (page 279) but add 1/4 c. cocoa to egg whites with flavorings.

Nutrients per serving:

Calories 20; Fat 0; Cholesterol 0; Sodium 12 mg;
Food exchange value: 1/2 fruit

Angels' Apricot Swirls

48 servings — 1 cookie each

1 1/4 c. all-purpose flour
1 c. potato flour (potato starch)
1/4 tsp. salt
1/2 c. reduced-fat sour cream
1/2 c. sugar
1/4 c. egg substitute
2 tsp. vanilla extract
1 tsp. grated lemon peel
Vegetable oil cooking spray
12 Tbsp. no-sugar-added apricot fruit spread,
    separated (3/4 c.)

Combine flours and salt in a large bowl; set aside. In a mixing bowl, beat together sour cream and sugar until creamy. Add egg substitute, vanilla extract, and lemon peel. Gradually stir in dry ingredients until combined. Wrap, and refrigerate overnight.

Preheat oven to 350°. Spray 2 cookie sheets with cooking spray.

Divide refrigerated dough in quarters. Work with one quarter of the dough at a time, keeping remaining quarters refrigerated. Roll each quarter into a 12- by 6-inch rectangle about 1/8-inch thick. Spread each rectangle with 3 tablespoons apricot spread, spreading all the way to the sides. Starting on long side, roll up rectangles, and place seam-side down on prepared baking sheet.

Bake for 15 to 17 minutes, or until bottom of rolls is just turning brown. Remove to a wire rack to cool for 10 to 15 minutes. While still slightly warm, slice each roll into 12 1-inch pieces. Place on a serving plate to complete cooling.

Nutrients per serving:
Calories 34; Fat 0; Cholesterol 0; Sodium 18 mg;
Food exchange value: 1/2 bread/starch

"We are ne'er like angels
till our passion dies."

-Thomas Dekker

Index